# INVINCIBLE
# JOY

Chasing God's Dreams for Your Life

## OLIVER L. ASHER

with Andrew Needham

**FREILING**
PUBLISHING

Bible versions used:

The Holy Bible, English Standard Version (ESV). ESV® Text Edition: 2016. Copyright © 2001 by Crossway Bibles, a publishing ministry of Good News Publishers.

The New King James Version® (NKJV). Copyright © 1982 by Thomas Nelson. Used by permission. All rights reserved.

The Holy Bible, New International Version®, NIV® Copyright © 1973, 1978, 1984, 2011 by Biblica, Inc.® Used by permission. All rights reserved worldwide.

Published by Freiling Publishing,
a division of Freiling Agency, LLC.

P.O. Box 1264
Warrenton, VA 20188

www.FreilingPublishing.com

PB ISBN: 978-1-956267-77-8
eBook ISBN: 978-1-956267-78-5

*Printed in the United States of America*

# Endorsements

I have known Oliver Asher for about sixteen years. He embodies "invincible joy." He always has a smile on his face. I had no idea of his story until he handed me this manuscript, which made his joy that much more remarkable. He lives the principle of this book. I heartily recommend *Invincible Joy*. Run, do not walk, to your bookstore or to Amazon to buy this book. You will be glad you did. I have a feeling you will read and reread it—like I am."

—Ruth Graham
Author of *Transforming Loneliness: Deepening Our Relationships With God and Others When We Feel Alone*

Do you want to experience Invincible Joy in your own life? Oliver's timely book touched my heart, drew me closer to God, and made me think about God's plans for my own life. Reading this book made me want to seize the moment to spend my life doing everything with a whole heart. Oliver is a godly and very humble man who exudes joy. This is his story of how God took him from extremely humble beginnings to be a leader and encourager of many. This book about his life will teach you how to find true joy in the midst of all circumstances. I highly recommend this book to those experiencing difficult times, those fighting depression, those who want to make their lives on this earth count for others, and those who want to live life to the fullest with Invincible Joy!

—Susan J. Brandt

Sr. Vice President Wealth Management, CFP, CRPC,

UBS Financial Services (Retired)

Listed in Barron's Top Female Financial Advisers

in the US

To read *Invincible Joy* is like finding a treasure in the field! It is a deeply moving and beautiful life story that the God who sees and hears gifted and entrusted to Oliver. That story becomes beyond beautiful when intertwined and wisely clad with apt and powerful scriptural lessons. The greatest value of this book is in finding its way into the hands and hearts of young men and women on a serious journey of finding their God-defined niche in the work of the kingdom. It's a book that one wishes to see on the big screen—in the likes of notable faith-based films produced by the Kendrick brothers, Alex and Stephen, that tug the heart-strings and end to the glory of our Almighty God and Savior Jesus Christ.

—Bo Barredo
Co-Founder of Advancing Native Missions
Author of *My Love Story with the God of Missions*

*Invincible Joy* is one man's story of his encounter with Jesus. It is a story of a man refined and heated in the fires of hardship, difficulties, disappointments, setbacks, and failures; a man called by the Lord, perfected by his faith, and nurtured by Jesus and the loving souls the Lord has surrounded him with.

It is also a story of love and the forming of a loving heart. The Lord has given Oliver a heart that loves others and loves to reach out to ask, dream, and accomplish all that the Lord has called him to do, for the glory of Jesus, until He returns.

As Oliver has seized today's moment to dream bigger dreams and to go and make disciples of all nations, may you also have Invincible Joy in the journey, abiding in the love of Jesus.

—Les Bell, Entrepreneur

# Contents

# Introduction

I DON'T KNOW where you were born, or what your family was like, or whether your family had a nice car or went on fancy vacations. I do know that God doesn't play favorites. He's not looking for the most prestigious family history or the greatest intellect or the most talented follower. He's looking for faithfulness.

If you drive a few miles out into the country from Damascus in southwest Virginia, at the foot of the Appalachian Mountains, go to the end of the paved road, turn onto the gravel road, and go to the end, you'll see where I grew up. It's just a bare patch of grass in the woods now. There's nothing left of the shack that was my home. But looking around at the woods, the creek, and the mountainside, you can still get the feel of what it was like. I didn't come from much.

In 1 Corinthians 1, the Apostle Paul writes, "Brothers and sisters, think of what you were when you were called. Not many of you were wise by human standards; not many were influential; not many were of noble birth. But God chose the foolish things of the world to shame the wise; God chose the weak things of the world to shame the strong. God chose the lowly things of this world and the despised things—and the things that are not—to nullify the things that are, so that no one may boast before him. It is because of him that you are in Christ Jesus, who has become for us wisdom from God—that is, our righteousness, holiness, and redemption. Therefore, as it is written: 'Let the one who boasts boast in the Lord.'"

So God will choose someone like me—you might call me a redneck, a hick, a hillbilly—who got a glimpse of God's grace and went looking for more. I'm not an extraordinary person. I came from next to nothing, from almost nowhere. But God had a plan and a purpose for my life. He picked me up from where I was and took me places I never could have expected to go. He invited me to join him in chasing his God-sized dreams for the world. And following him on that journey, through all the challenges and struggles, is where I found Invincible Joy.

You may have the same story. Or at least you can, and I hope you will. That's what this book is for. I didn't discover Invincible Joy overnight; it took many experiences, struggles, and hardships, and I'd love to share with you a few lessons the Lord has taught me over the years.

I'm not trying to give you all the answers, because I don't have them. Only God does. What you will find here are testimonies of the Lord's goodness, personal experiences through which the Lord showed me who he is and what his plans are for me, and a few nuggets of wisdom that I've received from God and from the influential people he has put in my life. I pray that you will benefit from all of this as you seek the Lord and follow him on your own adventure from where you came from to where he wants to take you. I believe, as the Lord leads, you will end up with a stronger sense of God's purpose for your life and your place in his plan for the world. That's where you can find Invincible Joy too.

Amen? Let's get started on the next page.

# 1

# A Chaotic Beginning

DAD BROKE OUT of prison a few months before I was born. His destination was Tampa, Florida, where Mom was living, pregnant with me. He was about twenty-two years old, and she was about sixteen.

They were poor kids from poor families. Dad was the oldest of twelve children and practically uneducated. Most his siblings spent time in jail—some of them more than once. Dad dropped out of school and left home around age fourteen or fifteen. One of the ways he made money was by stealing. Apparently, he was pretty good at it. He wasn't good enough to avoid getting caught before my birthday, though. He was hitchhiking back and forth from Florida to Maryland, breaking into houses along the way, and the police caught up with him.

He ended up in a prison camp in southern Florida, working on a chain gang. That was exactly what you might expect from movies you've seen—a bunch of men out along the roadway doing exhausting manual labor with armed guards watching. Dad had been there for a few months when he and a buddy decided to run for it. His buddy didn't make it far. He fell, and the guards found him and took him back in.

Dad escaped, though, and headed north. He trekked through a little obstacle called the Florida Everglades and kept going until he found Mom. For about three months, they hid out on a dairy farm near Tampa. Then someone tipped off the police that an escaped convict was living on the farm. As Mom and Dad tell the story, a SWAT team showed up to take him back. This time, they put Dad in a high-security prison for two years. He was in a dark four-by-eight cell for most of that time. That's where he was when I was born—his first child, named Oliver after him.

## A Less than Ideal Childhood

My earliest memory is from when I was about four years old. Dad was out of prison, and we were still living in the Tampa area. My parents would host all-night poker parties on Friday and Saturday nights. A few of their friends would come over, and they would drink and smoke and play cards all night and then go home. For a four-year-old boy, there was one really great thing about this: my parents' drunken friends lost track of their loose change during the night. In the morning, I went around collecting the change. Then I rode my bike down to the store and bought some one-cent candies.

After a few years together in Florida, Mom and Dad were looking for a fresh start. For our family, that fresh start was in southwest Virginia, where my dad's folks lived. So we moved to Virginia when I was five years old. For a while, we lived with Dad's parents. They were very poor. They lived along a creek in the woods in a trailer with rooms added on and some sheds in the yard. Grandpa had been a coal miner and was known to have a homemade moonshine still back in the mountains behind their homestead.

We moved into town for a little while. Then, when I was in third grade, my parents bought some land up the creek from my grandparents, outside of town up in Rush Creek Holler. In case you're not familiar with the Appalachian dialect, a "holler" is a small valley or low place between two hills on the edge of the mountains. There's usually a stream or creek running down the middle. As you might have guessed, it comes from the word "hollow," as in a hollow between two hills. Picture wooded mountains in a really rural area.

We were living what you might call the hillbilly life. Our home was a trailer in the woods. Dad did iron-working for the coal mines and whoever else had work available. Sometimes he had jobs that took him away for a while. We moved to Louisiana for several months when I was in third grade. All I remember about Louisiana were broken-down carnival rides in our front yard and a huge river behind our house. My brother, Danny, and I hunted lizards all day back there. I also spent some time doing gymnastics on my bunk bed. That resulted in a broken front tooth that didn't get capped until I was a senior in high school. We moved to Texas for a couple of months too. Soon after we arrived, I broke my leg playing football on the school playground and spent the rest of my time in Texas on crutches.

We were poor, but I didn't know that at the time. When you're in it—in any kind of difficult situation—you often don't realize it. It's just life.

There's a story about two fish swimming side by side in the ocean. One says, "Brr! The water's cold today."

The other one responds, "What's water?"

Our circumstances, and even our mindsets and habits, can be so familiar to us that we don't notice them or think carefully about them. But as you mature and receive wisdom from the Lord, you can gain a better understanding of yourself and the world around you. And you can, as the Apostle Paul says in Romans 12, "be transformed by the renewing of your mind."

## Which Is Real: Happy Social Media or Hopeless Hearts?

That was the beginning of my life. Kind of a rocky start, right? How does it compare with yours? Your dad might not have escaped from a chain gang. Your parents may or may not have been together during your early years. You might have had more or less financial security than we did. I believe this much is true about all of us, though: we're not born into an earthly paradise. Every single person on earth is born into a sinful, broken world in rebellion against God. And life is hard.

The list of hardships and struggles that people go through is endless. I'm sure that you know someone who has experienced each of these, even if you haven't yourself: serious illness, the death of a loved one, poverty, domestic violence, losing a job, divorce, a broken relationship with a sibling or close friend, war, hunger, or other challenges. In Romans 8:19–23, Paul says that all of creation is waiting and groaning in frustration. And we are too. Every one of us is groaning inside as we "wait eagerly" for redemption. Hopelessness, despair, and chaos are all around us.

People may post nothing but happy photos on their social media. In fact, their lives may look so great that it causes you to feel bad about your own. When you ask others in the office or at the coffee shop or even at church how they are doing, they will probably say, "Fine." Isn't that how it goes? The truth is, though, that people are lost, lonely, tired, and worried. Many of them do not have true hope, peace, or joy. And as you know from the seemingly endless list of self-help books, people have tried everything to fix what's wrong with them. This isn't one of those books, but I hope and pray that it will help you.

## What Can Carry You through It All?

There's something that can carry a person through all the chaos and darkness and troubles that the world will throw your way. Actually, it's a person—Jesus Christ. And I believe that when you walk with Jesus through the trials of this life, he gives you a kind of hope, peace, and joy that the world doesn't understand. That's what I've discovered, and I pray you'll see that in the chapters that follow. I like to sum it up with the phrase "Invincible Joy."

I first encountered Invincible Joy through the testimony of my grandma and my mom. Grandma couldn't read or write, but she knew and loved Jesus. She always wanted to talk about Jesus, and every conversation ended up about him. She was a stabilizing influence for our family.

When I was a kid, Grandma was an evangelist on the radio. Every day, she'd spend an hour or two in prayer and ask Grandpa to read the Bible to her. Sometimes in her prayer time, the Lord would give her a word or a message, and she would ask Grandpa to find it in the Bible. She just knew it was in there. One time she was praying and the Lord gave her the phrase, "New creation." She told Grandpa, "I know it's in there. Find it for me." So he found 2 Corinthians 5:17, and she spoke on that passage on her radio program.

When my family moved from Florida to Virginia, neither my mom nor my dad was saved. When I was in elementary school, maybe six or seven years old, Grandma shared the Good News of Jesus with Mom. Mom shared the Good News with me and my brother, Danny, who was three years younger than I was. Then she started taking us to church. I didn't understand a lot about the Christian faith at the time, but I knew that I was a sinner and that I needed Jesus. As I started to follow him under the guidance of Mom and Grandma, I started to see hope. I also started to dream of doing something for the Lord. For me, that also meant doing something for the Asher name that was different from what had come in the generations before. Mom was the biggest influence in my life and is still the person most like Jesus I've ever known.

Who has been that Christlike influence for you? Have you experienced joy in the midst of hardship?

# 2

## Suffering Is Inevitable

LIFE IS EASY, right?

No! Of course, there are times and seasons when you might say that. But you may have to wait only a few days or a few hours to encounter one of the obstacles, barriers, or opposing forces that the world throws in front of you. We are very good at forgetting hardship and remembering and expecting the good times.

If you've been through childbirth as a mom, you intimately understand what I'm talking about. From everything I've heard and experienced secondhand, pregnancy and giving birth are not easy. But the pain and discomfort tend to fade after you hold that newborn baby, watch your son or daughter sleeping in the crib, and see him or her grow up before your eyes. Maybe that forgetfulness is a divine mercy to help parents go for another child after experiencing the pain and discomfort of childbirth. My wife, Andrea, and I have five kids!

The truth is that life is hard and suffering is inevitable. Jesus makes this very clear in John 16:33, where he says, "In this world you will have trouble." What a promise! You can't avoid suffering, no matter how much the American culture insists that you can. It's not a matter of how to avoid suffering; it's a matter of how to redeem it. As I suggested in the last chapter, everything changes when we walk through suffering with the Lord. Our mindset can be renewed and transformed by the Holy Spirit so we can actually experience blessing and joy in suffering.

That's easier said than done. It's one of the hardest lessons to learn, and it's best if we can learn it early in life. I want to share one episode from my life that taught me something about hardship and how we respond to it.

## The Worst Thing That Could Have Happened

In 1978, I turned twelve and started seventh grade. The year was off to a good start. Things were going well at home. My dad had steady work. Then, on November 30, something happened that I still remember vividly today. It was the early afternoon, and I was in English class when I was called to the school office. I was generally a good kid, so I knew something was up. The vice principal, Mr. Arnold, ushered me into his office and offered me a seat. He sat down and looked at me with the kind of serious look that puts a little fear into your heart. You know what I mean? What he said next was worse than I could have imagined.

"Oliver, I hate to tell you this, but your house burned down."

My first thought, of course, was about my mom. "Was Mom at home? Is she all right?"

Mr. Arnold relieved those fears right away. "Your mom is okay. She was able to get out in time."

Evidently, it started in the wood stove. A coal must have fallen out at some point. Mom was taking a nap in the other room when she woke suddenly, smelling smoke. The fire spread quickly to the entire trailer. She got out, but our home was gone. Mr. Arnold tried to comfort me and told me that someone had once told him, "This too shall pass." He said that had comforted him, and he hoped it would comfort me. I'll never forget that.

For some reason, they didn't send me home right then. I stayed at school and finished my classes, and then I got on the school bus to ride home. As you can imagine, that bus ride was almost unbearable. It was about ten miles to get home. I remember coming around that last bend before the house. There's a bit of a decline there, and I remember coming down and around that last curve and seeing the trailer in shambles—blackened, melted, and almost completely consumed. My home was gone.

My grandparents lived a few hundred yards up the road, so after the bus dropped me off, I walked up to their trailer. The rest of that day is kind of fuzzy in my memory. We stayed with my grandparents for a short while. Then in December, we moved into what I always called the "toolshed." It was, just as it sounds, a shed where we stored tools and other things. It sat up the slope a couple of hundred yards from where the trailer had been. It was poorly built out of scrap lumber, and you could literally see through the cracks in the walls to the outside. Basically, it was just the shell of a building: no interior walls, no running water, no bathroom. One light bulb hung in the middle of the room. We had an outhouse on the side of the hill. I bathed in the creek during the warmer months and showered at the school when it got colder.

That first winter was so cold. Whatever the temperature was outside, that's what it was inside. I remember even having some snow in our bedroom sometimes. Through the cracks in the floorboards, we could see the chickens running under the shed to keep warm. We put up cardboard that first winter to keep at least a little of the cold out. Thank God for Mom, who would get up in the night and feed the wood stove and wake in the morning to make us breakfast. She was awesome.

Mom and Dad decided they would save up some money and buy another trailer eventually. Six months was the plan. But we ended up living in the shed for six years. We divided the single room into four: a living room, a kitchen, a bedroom for my parents and my sister, and a bedroom for me and my brother. Eventually we added a bathroom, putting in a pipe to run cold water to the shed from a spring about a quarter of a mile away.

There's one other memory related to this episode of my life that I want to share with you, just to show that the experiences of our lives have ripple effects, and sometimes they are surprising. The year our trailer burned, things were going well for our family. My dad had steady work, and we felt that we were "in high cotton," as the old saying goes. My parents had actually bought Christmas presents for us and saved them in a closet in the trailer. They disappeared in the flames. After that, my dad never saved a present. As soon as he bought one, he would give it to us.

I'm thankful that my mom had shared the Gospel with me by this time because it helped me through this difficult season. I knew that the Lord was watching out for us and that he had a purpose for us. I already had a deep conviction that God had something in mind for me to do. Again, Jesus said, "In this world you will have trouble." And the very next thing he said was, "But take heart! I have overcome the world." All the trouble of the world has been overcome already. There is always some kind of redemption in the hardship.

## What to Do When You Encounter Hardships

Life isn't all celebration. So the question to ask yourself is "How do I look at a problem or a challenge?" I'm naturally an optimist, so my personality leads me to look at problems as opportunities. I also have experienced enough difficulties through which the Lord has taught me an important lesson: We grow through challenges. The important thing is recognizing the purpose and potential outcomes of our challenges, sufferings, and problems. I've found James 1:2–4 to be incredibly helpful in this:

*Count it all joy, my brothers, when you meet trials of various kinds, for you know that the testing of your faith produces steadfastness. And let steadfastness have its full effect, that you may be perfect and complete, lacking in nothing. (ESV)*

You can get hung up on your circumstances, or you can focus on your character. Circumstances are generally out of your control. Yes, you have the free will to make decisions about your actions and your mindset, and that's all very important. But unexpected things are also going to happen to you. You can't just raise your hand and say, "Excuse me, I didn't sign up for this!" What you can do is decide how your circumstances will shape your character.

That's called joy: knowing that the Lord is working everything out for your good through every circumstance. Here are just a few of my recent opportunities to "count it all joy" in my life:

- A gullywasher (that's what we called an intense storm where I grew up) flooded the basement in our new home right after we moved in.

- I received a call from a longtime missions partner who told me he was going to partner with a different organization.

- My daughter called, excited about twins, then a few weeks later called again to say that there was now only one baby.

- One of my dear friends passed away unexpectedly.

- I prepared our yard for new grass, sowed the seed at the right time, fertilized it, covered it with straw, and watered it religiously, but then the wind blew it all away, leaving a yard of red clay.

- Our team at work put in our best effort, everything was running smoothly, and we expected the best results ever, but then we found out that we were doing 30 percent worse than last year.

I'm sure you could share your own list. James is speaking from experience too. He endured persecution, the loss of friends and fellow disciples, disputes within the church, and of course the loss of his brother and Lord, Jesus. Yet he tells us to count it all joy because he witnessed the outcome. Indeed, he experienced it himself. When we suffer in faith and count it all joy, we become "perfect and complete, lacking in nothing." In other words, it makes us more like Jesus, right?

I want to share Romans 5:1–5 with you as well:

*Therefore, having been justified by faith, we have peace with God through our Lord Jesus Christ, through whom also we have access by faith into this grace in which we stand, and rejoice in hope of the glory of God. And not only that, but we also glory in tribulations, knowing that tribulation produces perseverance; and perseverance, character; and character, hope. Now hope does not disappoint, because the love of God has been poured out in our hearts by the Holy Spirit who was given to us. (NKJV)*

Isn't that wonderful? We see that progression from suffering to endurance to character to hope. Suffering ends up in hope, and hope doesn't disappoint. Often the hardest times lead to the greatest joys. How do we know that? Because we know that God is at work.

Whatever you have in front of you today, you can know that the challenge, problem, or suffering you are facing will end up in hope. You are a child of God, and he

will make sure that whatever you are going through will result in your good.

I want to close with Hebrews 12:1-2, which shows us the mindset of our Savior as he endured the trials of this life and the ultimate suffering of the cross:

> *Therefore, since we are surrounded by so great a cloud of witnesses, let us also lay aside every weight, and sin which clings so closely, and let us run with endurance the race that is set before us, looking to Jesus, the founder and perfecter of our faith, who for the joy that was set before him endured the cross, despising the shame, and is seated at the right hand of the throne of God.*

Jesus left his throne to endure physical pain, spiritual and emotional pain, rejection, abandonment, a fake trial, ridicule, torture, and crucifixion. Why? For joy.

18

# 3

## Invincible Joy Can Be Found in the Midst of Trouble

I WAS SIXTEEN years old and a sophomore in high school. We were living in the toolshed, which we had improved and added onto by that time. My brother, Danny, is about three years behind me, and my sister, Missy, about three years younger than Danny. We were all sharing life in that little shack.

My girlfriend invited me over to her house, and I couldn't drive yet. The only way I could get there was for Mom or Dad to drive me there. So that day, we all drove over in our truck, everyone except Danny. I had been at their house for a short time when my girlfriend's dad came over and told me we needed to go. He was going to take me home early. He owned a police radio scanner, and although I didn't know it at the time, I suspect he already knew what had happened.

We arrived at my house, and I remember getting out of their car and seeing Mom and Dad with these contorted facial expressions. It was dark and hard to see. I asked what happened, and Dad told me, "Oliver, Missy's dead." On their way back from dropping me off at my girlfriend's house, there had been a car accident, and Missy had died.

Everything went dark in that moment. All I could say was "What? What are you talking about?" I remember that pain even now. We were all just standing around crying out to God for that special girl with the long blond hair, freckled nose, and sky blue eyes. She was a bright light, always smiling, always with a song in her heart, bringing joy to all of us. It was just ten days before her ninth birthday.

Of course, then the guilt came. If I hadn't asked to be driven to my girlfriend's house, this wouldn't have happened. I struggled with that for a while. Over time, talking to my mom, I found peace. She told me, "This is not your fault." My dad had become a Christian just before that. To see how God kept him and my mom during that time helped me. I saw the peace and calm that God was giving them. I know that if Dad had still been drinking and living the hard life, he could have gone off the deep end. That was God's mercy for me through them.

It seems as though all of us had special times with Missy in the two weeks or so before her death, and we held onto those. I think of laughing together and enjoying the moments together with that sweet girl. Sometimes Missy would sing on Grandma's radio program. I remembered hearing her singing country gospel songs when she was just four, five, or six years old.

How do you make it through something like that?

## Transformed by Suffering

All of us experience deep sorrows and pains in our lives. When you walk with Jesus, that experience is different. A deep, intimate relationship with the Lord causes us to be transformed by suffering as the Lord redeems those experiences in our lives. It's not an immediate thing. It doesn't erase the suffering. Remembering Missy now still brings me to tears. But somehow, the Lord strengthened me through that loss, even as he softened my heart through it too. That's Invincible Joy.

How do you define joy? Is it like happiness? Or is it something more? St. Augustine of Hippo once wrote, "How sweet all at once it was for me to be rid of those fruitless joys which I had once feared to lose! ... You drove them from me, you who are the true, the sovereign joy. You drove them from me and took their place ... O Lord my God, my Light, my Wealth, and my Salvation."

He's talking about the joys that fill our lives that aren't real joys. They are fruitless, meaning that they take up space but don't add lasting value or benefit. This is the kind of joy that you might tell your friend about in a light conversation, but if you took the time to really think about it honestly, you might not call it joy.

"I've been so busy at work." We brag about that, don't we?

"I got to sleep in this morning." This might be a small pleasure, but is it joy?

"I was finally invited to join that group for their weekly lunch." We often look for our value in the wrong places, building our lives on a shifting foundation. Is that joy?

Invincible Joy is stronger, is more lasting, and doesn't depend on circumstances. It doesn't run away when things get tough. It doesn't fade a few minutes after something good happens. In fact, it gets stronger as our circumstances seem to get worse. It shines in our darkest moments. It supports us when we feel most vulnerable and weak. Like love, it's a commitment. When you get up in the morning and it's raining and there's too much on the calendar and the bills are overdue, you can say, "This is the day that the Lord has made. I'm going to rejoice and be glad in it."

## What Does Invincible Joy Look Like?

Let's look at a biblical character who experienced Invincible Joy.

Nehemiah was leading the people of Israel through a difficult season. He had returned from exile to rebuild Jerusalem. The small community of Jews seemed weak, and they were surrounded by enemies. There were even enemies among them. They faced a humongous task: rebuilding the walls, protecting themselves and their work from their enemies, and bringing life back to the city.

Perhaps most important of all, they were out of touch with who they were. They had been scattered and exiled. They had lost many of their traditions and their knowledge of the scriptures. When they gathered to hear the scriptures read, they wept because they realized how far they had drifted from the Lord. And that's where Nehemiah introduced them to Invincible Joy.

He and the other leaders reminded the people of the Lord's love for them and his covenant with them. And Nehemiah invited them to come closer to the Lord and literally camp out in his presence. He said, "Go and enjoy choice food and sweet drinks, and send some to those who have nothing prepared. This day is holy to our Lord. Do not grieve, for the joy of the LORD is your strength."

Then he and Ezra instructed them to gather materials to build temporary shelters and celebrate the Feast of Booths (Tabernacles or Tents) for the first time since the days of Joshua. Remember, this was a small group of people who had been through exile and had come home to a ruined city. They had put in a huge amount of work, but the city was nothing to be proud of from an outsider's point of view. You wouldn't have called it glorious. The people around them probably mocked their work. But as the Jews drew close to the Lord together, they experienced something better than the praise of their neighbors or the temporary glory of work accomplished or the pleasure of possessions and wealth. Nehemiah 8:17 says, "Their joy was very great."

This is where we really see how the joy of the Lord, Invincible Joy, is different from the fleeting "joys" that the world offers us, because this Invincible Joy isn't just happiness. It includes three foundational qualities: an unshakable faith in the Father our provider, an unshakable love for Jesus our Savior, and an unshakable hope in the future.

You might recognize those three qualities from 1 Corinthians 13. The Apostle Paul says that after everything else has passed away and faded, "These three remain: faith, hope, and love. But the greatest of these is love." Some theologians refer to these as the "Theological Virtues." I like to think of them as the three layers that undergird Invincible Joy. Together, these three keep us steady and firm in Christ.

The first is an unshakable faith in the Father, our provider. Let's unpack that a little. One scripture passage that comes to my mind when I consider this is Matthew 6:25–34, from the Sermon on the Mount:

> *Therefore I tell you, do not worry about your life, what you will eat or drink; or about your body, what you will wear. Is not life more than food, and the body more than clothes? Look at the birds of the air; they do not sow or reap or store away in barns, and yet your heavenly Father feeds them. Are you*

*not much more valuable than they? Can any one of you by worrying add a single hour to your life?*

*And why do you worry about clothes? See how the flowers of the field grow. They do not labor or spin. Yet I tell you that not even Solomon in all his splendor was dressed like one of these. If that is how God clothes the grass of the field, which is here today and tomorrow is thrown into the fire, will he not much more clothe you—you of little faith? So do not worry, saying, "What shall we eat?" or "What shall we drink?" or "What shall we wear?" For the pagans run after all these things, and your heavenly Father knows that you need them. But seek first his kingdom and his righteousness, and all these things will be given to you as well. Therefore do not worry about tomorrow, for tomorrow will worry about itself. Each day has enough trouble of its own.*

With these simple illustrations, Jesus shows the people listening to him that God is aware of our needs. Because God is sovereign and because God designed and created us (and the birds and the flowers), he understands who we are and what we need. We also see that God is able to provide: God has providentially arranged it so that the birds and the flowers have everything they need to grow and glorify him. He is able to send rain when the flowers need it. He is able to send food for the birds. And he is able to supply food, clothes, and everything else you and I need. Jesus also shows us that God cares. He isn't just observing us from a distance. He loves as the perfect father loves his children. Isn't it amazing how Jesus calls God your "Heavenly Father"? Jesus is inviting the people to see God as their father and to see themselves as part of God's family. A father isn't some distant ruler who watches from afar. He sits with his children, invites them to the table with him, and rejoices in their presence. That's the kind of God we have.

The next foundation of Invincible Joy is an unshakable love for Jesus our Savior. We just have to look at what our lovely Savior has done for us to understand this. He gave everything so that we could be forgiven and be included in the Lord's family. Philippians 2:5–8 is just one of the many scripture passages that illustrate this for me:

*In your relationships with one another, have the same mindset as Christ Jesus, who, being in very nature God, did not consider equality with God something to be used to his own advantage; rather, he made himself nothing by taking the very nature of a servant, being made in human likeness. And being found in appearance as a man, he humbled himself by becoming obedient to death—even death on a cross!*

Jesus had everything! He was God, and he was on the throne of heaven, but he emptied himself to become a helpless baby, to suffer all the discomforts and pains and frustrations that we suffer, to serve, and ultimately to be tortured and killed for our sins. 2 Corinthians 5:21 says, "God made him who had no sin to be sin for us, so that in him we might become the righteousness of God."

Now that's love! And it inspires love in your heart and mine. I understand that sometimes we can start to become jaded and forget our passion for the Lord. That's why it's so important to turn back to scriptures like these and just be reminded of the Lord's love for us and of what he has done for us. I encourage you to make a list of some of the Bible verses that remind you of that love. Read them in the morning, and memorize them so you can repeat them to yourself throughout the day. Say them before you go to sleep at night. Our hearts need those kinds of reminders to keep our love kindled.

The third foundation of Invincible Joy is an unshakable hope in the future. The world thinks of hope as something like a wish. Think about it: we might say, "I hope it doesn't rain" or "I hope the Cavaliers win the game today." But hope is so much deeper than that, and it's so much more powerful. It can actually transform us from the inside. Hope can affect our attitudes and actions. It can change what we say to ourselves and what we say to others.

For me, the most powerful biblical message of hope is in Romans 8. The whole chapter speaks about who we are in Christ. I'll share just a few of the "greatest hits" from this chapter:

Verse 1: "Therefore, there is now no condemnation for those who are in Christ Jesus."

Verse 28: "And we know that in all things God works for the good of those who love him, who have been called according to his purpose."

Verse 31: "If God is for us, who can be against us?"

And of course, Verse 37, one of my favorite verses of all time: "No, in all these things we are more than conquerors through him who loved us."

Aren't these powerful messages of hope for God's people? We have an amazing assurance that God has arranged everything for our good. The God of the universe is for you. There is reason to be hopeful.

To sum up, these three foundations hold up our Invincible Joy: unshakable faith, unshakable love, and unshakable hope. These three things work together to help us stand joyfully through all the situations we go through in this life. I want to conclude by encouraging you with this: The joy of the Lord is accessible, it is sufficient, and it is everlasting. Finally—and you know this—the joy of the Lord is better than any brief happiness, pleasure, or comfort the world offers.

# 4

# Dreams Get You Moving
# Toward the Lord

WHAT WAS YOUR childhood dream? Become an astronaut? Travel the world? Star in a movie?

For me, it was to play professional football. My training started early, but it wasn't the kind of training you might expect. Dad was always a hard worker. When my parents decided to move to Rush Creek Holler near my grandparents, they somehow purchased about sixty acres of woodland with the idea that we could cut and sell firewood to supplement Dad's income.

Dad and my brother, Danny, and I would load Dad's four-wheel-drive truck with our chainsaws and axes. We drove up the rough road he had cleared into the woods, and we spent the day logging. Usually, Dad cut down the tree, I cut it up, and Danny trimmed it. We would load the wood into the back of the truck and drive it down to the trailer. We had a ten-pound maul that Danny and I would use to bust up the wood into firewood for the winter. Dad would drive us around the neighborhoods of Abingdon with a truckload of firewood and a "Firewood for Sale" sign.

The work didn't stop when it snowed. Sometimes in the winter, we would go up and cut wood in six inches of snow. Danny and I didn't have gloves, so we wore socks on our hands. Of course, those got wet almost immediately in the snow. It was a cold experience. If we couldn't get the truck to where we were working, we would just cut the wood. Then Danny and I would take the bigger pieces and roll them down the stream bed to the bottom of the mountain. The smaller pieces we would throw. It was kind of a game: Who can roll or throw the log the farthest? Isn't it amazing how kids can make anything into a game?

Looking back now, it was a different world. My kids would totally not relate. I remember one time I was sawing a limb too fast and the chainsaw came down suddenly on my leg, ripped through my pants, and cut a gash in my leg. I just ripped a strip of cloth from my shirt, tied it around my leg to stop the bleeding, and went back to work. That was just life for us. Danny and I were helping Mom and Dad earn a living and put food on the table. I once asked Dad what our most productive woodcutting day was. He told me we once cut and hauled twenty-seven truckloads of wood in a single day. You can see how I was ready for football workouts.

## From Failure to Success

My high school was seventh through twelfth grade, a little over 400 kids. In seventh grade, I went out for the seventh and eighth grade football team, the Holston Cavaliers. Our varsity team was a perennial loser. I think they had four winning seasons in twenty years. The year before I started, the varsity Cavaliers had won two games. My eighth grade year, they played our rivals, the Chilhowie Warriors, and were totally annihilated. I didn't see the game, but I heard about it from all of my friends. They said it seemed that Chilhowie scored every time they had the ball, and Chilhowie scored every time we had the ball. Late in the fourth quarter, it was 91–0. The whole crowd—including our own fans—started chanting, "One hundred! One hundred!" Everyone wanted to see what would happen to our two-digit scoreboard when Chilhowie passed 100. They didn't make it, but it was an ugly game. Our coach got fired the next day.

That's where our program was when I started. My sophomore year, we went 2–8. Not so great, but we were a very young team. The following year, we won eight games and lost two. We ended up second in the district. Then my senior year, we won the district championship for the first time in school history. By the way, we played our rivals again and still lost, but only 7–6 this time.

My pro football dream really took shape during those years. I was playing linebacker, and by my junior year, everything was clicking. I could see my future laid out ahead of me: I would win a starting position on a college team, succeed at that level, get drafted, and enjoy a successful career as a pro athlete. My dream also included blessing those who had blessed me in my life, especially Mom. I was going to buy her a new house. There would also be a little something for me: a red Corvette looked great in my fantasy driveway. Looking back now, some of that seems childish and unrealistic. But God used that dream to spur me on. I worked hard, and I grew up as a man under the leadership of godly coaches. And God paved the way for me to go to college.

Our new coach, Coach Alderman, saw my potential and was a great encouragement. He was an awesome, godly man, and he really mentored and guided me during those last two years of school. And he was an advocate for me. College coaches don't typically come recruiting at 400-student schools in the middle of nowhere, especially back then. There's a lot of talent out there, but if you're not at the right school, you could go unnoticed. Coach Alderman helped me send some tapes to colleges so I could get noticed. It was really a miracle for me to be recruited from there. I wish you could have witnessed the scene when the coaches from the University of Virginia showed up at our shack in the holler with the papers for me to play football there on a scholarship.

In July 1984, I was living in a shack in a holler in the mountains. In August I moved into a first-year dorm at the University of Virginia in Charlottesville. Talk about culture shock, and not just from backwoods country to sophisticated college town. I'm talking about some of the basics: Suddenly I had a comfortable bed, a bathroom, air conditioning, and heating. I ate all kinds of awesome food in the dining halls. And ate, and ate, and ate. When you're doing two grueling football practices a day in August, you work up an appetite.

My first year, our team—also called the Cavaliers— won eight out of twelve regular-season games and went to the school's first-ever bowl game. We arrived in Atlanta in late December for the Peach Bowl and had a police escort for our charter buses as we drove around the city. We stayed in five-star hotels. We hit every hot-spot in the city. I was living the dream. That's what I thought at the time, anyway. Obviously that dream was largely about worldly things and my own success, but that doesn't mean God wasn't using it to take me where he wanted me to go. Looking back now, even my football dream fits into what I've learned about God and his dreams for his people and the world.

## What to Do When Your Dream Dies

Have you experienced the death of a dream? As a child, you dreamed all the time: what you were going to be when you grew up, what kind of house you'd live in, who you'd marry, or which position you'd play in the pros. But as we grow up, we go through something that's really tough. We experience some setbacks that cause us to question and doubt. You have probably experienced the feeling that you must have been mistaken about one particular dream or another. That leads to an uncomfortable truth: Sometimes dreams die. During my third year at UVA, my football dream died a painful death.

When you play a sport in college, especially football, you don't play very much your first and second year. That's expected. Your third year is when you might get a chance. I practiced hard my first two years and mostly watched the games from the sidelines. I held out hope that my dream would come true. During the summer after my second year, though, I learned that I wasn't going to be traveling with the team for away games in the fall. If I was going to have my moment, this was it, and it looked as if it wasn't going to happen.

The truth is that maybe one out of a hundred high school players will get a scholarship to play on a Division I college team. Only about one out of a hundred college players gets drafted by an NFL team. Most of those pro players aren't stars. On average, pro football players last only a few years in the league. But I had been convinced that it would all come together for me in a stellar career.

Sometimes that happens, right? You focus like a laser on your dream, everything else disappears, and then one day something jars your attention. You look around and realize that everything's not the way you expected or hoped. That reality check was devastating for me, to the point that I almost failed out of school the first semester of my third year. My thought was, *If I can't even get playing time, what am I doing here?*

That was an identity crisis. I was a football player. That's who I was. I had been eating, drinking, and living the football dream since middle school. It was my ticket out of the hillbilly life. It was how I was going to bless my mom. And then there was that red Corvette ...

I bet you've had one of those "What am I even doing here?" moments. Or several of them. I believe we all come to these pivotal moments in our lives when we let go of a dream. More often than not, it feels as if that dream is ripped from our hands—or our hearts. Usually that leads to some soul searching. When everything seems upside down all of a sudden, when the bottom has fallen out of your dream, when you're not sure who you are and what you're supposed to do, there's one question you have to ask: "God, what are you doing in my life?"

So I asked the Lord, and after a time of agonizing soul searching and prayer, I received three answers. Number one: I had met a beautiful young lady named Andrea during my first year of college. God had put us together, and we were planning to get married after graduation. Number two: I was going to graduate with a great degree from an amazing university. I was the first person in my family to get a college degree. That degree would open doors for years to come. And number three: I was involved in a local church, and I loved it. On Sunday mornings, Andrea and I drove the van around town, picking up elderly ladies who needed a ride to church. For part of that time, I had a mohawk haircut—part of my 1980s UVA football style—which I'm sure was a shock to some of them. We also helped out with the teenagers at church as youth leaders.

## God Might Not Give You Answers, But . . .

God didn't exactly answer my "Why can't I be a professional football player?" question. He didn't exactly answer my questions about what the use of all that hard work and dedication had been. He didn't tell me exactly what I was going to do next. He didn't promise me that I would find another way to buy Mom a house or to get a Corvette.

Isn't that often how it goes? God doesn't fill in all the details we're looking for. He invites us to follow him in a new direction. The other thing he does is actually to transform us from the inside out in the process.

I think of Job in the Bible, who endured so many trials and lost almost everything. He believed he was righteous in spite of his friends' accusations and doubts. He continued in his faith in God, but he also questioned him.

In the end, God appeared to Job and spoke with him. God didn't really answer Job's questions. Instead, he displayed his power and glory and sovereignty to Job. Then Job responded with humility and worship: "I know that you can do all things; no purpose of yours can be thwarted.... Surely I spoke of things I did not understand, things too wonderful for me to know.... My ears had heard of you, but now my eyes have seen you. Therefore I despise myself and repent in dust and ashes." Then the beautiful moment came where God vindicated Job. He still didn't answer all of his questions, but he told Job's friends that he was pleased with Job and not with them. He lifted up Job in their eyes and asked him to pray for his friends. Then he restored Job's fortunes. Job 42:12 says, "The LORD blessed the latter part of Job's life more than the former part."

Job didn't get answers; he got an amazing encounter with the Lord that we're still reading about today. He got a heart that was humble and worshipful. And the Lord gave him a fresh start in life.

For me, when God gave me those three messages in response to my question, he really gave me one amazing gift: I understood that I was more than a football player. Football was a blessing. It got me to where I was at that time. But that season was ending. God had something else in store for me. So I basically told God, "Okay, Lord. I give up my dream to you." That's the kind of lesson we learn over and over again in our lives. What we have been through and who we have been are good, but that is not all we are or all we have. Our past and our past dreams are not wasted, either. I like to say that God never wastes anything we go through. In fact, one of my favorite verses in the Bible is Romans 8:28 where Paul says, "And we know that in all things God works for the good of those who love him, who have been called according to his purpose." Through every victory and every defeat, every dream and every death of a dream, God is doing something good for you.

That's where dreaming ties into Invincible Joy. God may give you a dream for a season. That dream is what spurs you on to follow the Lord into the unknown, where you experience Invincible Joy—life with God when you don't have all the answers. Chasing a dream is actually just the beginning—it's what gets you out of your comfort zone and into pursuit of the Lord who has an even bigger dream for your life.

Can you recall a dream or a season of life that ended painfully for you? I encourage you to ask the Lord a few honest questions about it: "What good came out of that?" "What are you doing in my life now?" "What's next?" Sometimes we have to wait for the answer to become clear. It may even be years later when you'll look back at an experience or a season of life and realize that the Lord used it to prepare you for something in the future.

# 5

# God Is the Biggest Dreamer

I BELIEVE DREAMING is a sacred thing. In fact, I like to call God the greatest dreamer. If you look at the scriptures, you'll see that our God is a God of dreams and visions. Here are a few examples.

In Genesis 28, God gives Jacob a dream of a stairway or ladder going up to heaven. Angels are climbing up and down the ladder. And God makes Jacob a promise in that dream:

> I am the LORD, the God of your father Abraham and the God of Isaac. I will give you and your descendants the land on which you are lying. Your descendants will be like the dust of the earth, and you will spread out to the west and to the east, to the north and to the south. All peoples on earth will be blessed through you and your offspring. I am with you and will watch over you wherever you go, and I will bring you back to this land. I

*will not leave you until I have done what I have*
*promised you.*

In Genesis 37, Joseph has two dreams that show him how the Lord will bless him among his brothers. As you probably know, those dreams also get him into some trouble with his brothers. Later, Joseph, who was wrongly imprisoned, is given freedom and authority because he interprets the dreams of his fellow prisoners and ultimately the dreams of Pharaoh. God transformed Joseph's character and his circumstances through those dreams and made him a blessing to many people.

In Acts 10, God gives Peter a vision that is actually a glimpse of God's own dream for the church. Peter sees, coming down from heaven, something like a sheet full of animals that the Jews considered clean and unclean. God tells Peter, "Do not call anything impure that God has made clean." Of course, he's talking about the Gentiles God is bringing into the church along with the Jews.

There are countless other examples too. The point is that God has plans for his people, and he gives us dreams and visions to reveal his plans, to shine the light on the truth, and to show his people what he wants to do in their lives. God is always prompting us to look toward the future and see where he wants us to go next. Waiting is an important part of the life of a believer; getting comfortable isn't. God takes us on a journey in this life, and dreams help lead the way.

## The Biggest Dream of All

God also has a dream that stretches larger and grander than all of the other dreams in scripture. He gives Abraham a glimpse of this dream in Genesis 12: "I will make you into a great nation, and I will bless you; I will make your name great, and you will be a blessing. I will bless those who bless you, and whoever curses you I will curse; and all peoples on earth will be blessed through you."

That's the grand dream that God is dreaming for his creation, and that's the dream we see playing out and coming to fruition throughout the Bible. God takes Abraham and gives him a family, even though he and Sarah are well beyond child-bearing age. He calls and preserves a people for himself and rescues them from slavery in Egypt. He carves out a place for them among the nations as a witness. Then he sends his Son as Savior and king of a people that will one day include all the nations of the earth. And he uses his church to bring the nations to himself.

Finally, in Revelation 7, we see the culmination of God's dream, where the Apostle John witnesses "a great multitude that no one could count, from every nation, tribe, people, and language, standing before the throne and before the Lamb."

So you see, God is a dreamer. He envisions what can be and what will be, and he invites us to move toward that vision with him. That's where we find fulfillment. We're really designed to catch God's vision and chase it with him. I believe God continues to bless his people with dreams and visions that give us glimpses of the way forward and the path God has laid out for us. They encourage us to walk forward in faith. They inspire us, as William Carey famously said, "to expect big things of God and attempt great things for God."

I encourage you not to discount the dreams you dream, whether as a high schooler or as a grandparent— even the ones with red Corvettes. Hidden inside those dreams may be the path God has laid out for you for this season. That's where his blessing for you may lie, as it did for Jacob. He also will use that dream to bless others through you, as he did through Joseph. Hold your dreams as sacred. Give God thanks for the vision he has given you, commit yourself to it, and see where it takes you.

What dream has God put into your heart?

# 6

## Two Questions to Ask When Seeking the Lord's Direction

MY FOURTH YEAR of college ended up being my best. I was at peace. The NFL dream was gone, but I did get to travel with the team. I played in most of the games and earned my varsity letter. My first away game was "between the hedges" on the famous home field of the Georgia Bulldogs in Athens, playing in front of 80,000 people. That's a memory I will never forget. More importantly, my relationship with Andrea flourished. She had come to faith in Jesus in college. I proposed to her, and we started to look ahead to life after college.

The Lord had been so good to us. We wanted to do something together to show our gratitude. Two questions began to form in my heart as we sought the Lord's will. The first question was: "What next, Lord?" One dream had died, but there is always something next. The Lord is always inviting us to dream big with him and open our hearts and minds to the possibilities that may be in store for us. The other key question to ask to engage in what the Lord is doing in your life is, "How can I serve you, Lord?" I've found that those two questions prepare us for a life of adventure with the Lord. It's amazing to me to stop and think that God invites us to follow him through the twists and turns of life, and to be part of his transformation of the world in the process. What a privilege!

## Going on an Adventure with the Lord

As Andrea and I prayed about our future, our hearts were both drawn to overseas missions. It happened that our pastor's sister and brother-in-law were serving as missionaries in the Dominican Republic. They invited us to come down after we graduated. So we decided to spend the first year of our marriage doing missions work.

Now, I've been asked many times whether it was a good idea to go to the mission field immediately after getting married. Honestly, I'm not sure I would recommend it. You're just getting used to your spouse during that first year of marriage, and then all of sudden you're in a new culture with a new language. You can always go to the mission field in year two or later. It definitely was God's will for us, though.

We embarked on that journey with grateful hearts. We needed something like $450 per month of financial support, and that was quickly taken care of by our local church and others. We got married in June, and by August we were in the Dominican Republic. We started out in the capital city, Santo Domingo, helping to construct a church building and serving in the church. Then we moved into the interior of the country to work on some other projects.

The Dominican Republic was a season, not a career. Andrea and I knew that going in. Ten months later, we were packing up and moving back to the States. The Lord put it in our hearts to return to Charlottesville, where we had been in school and where we had started our relationship. We didn't know what was next. We only knew who was leading us, and that gave us incredible peace as we looked into the unknown.

## How to Have Joy in Periods of Uncertainty

During that season, I was just getting my bearings. Andrea and I knew the Lord had plans for us, and we were gratefully serving him as we also grew closer together and became a family. After a miscarriage early in our marriage, Andrea was pregnant with our oldest son, Oliver Alexander, when we arrived back home from the Dominican Republic. God was keeping us on our toes!

As I mentioned before, we sensed early on that the Lord was calling us into full-time ministry. At the time, we believed every Christian felt that way. I realized over time, though, that Christians are called to serve the Lord in many different ways. That full-time ministry path isn't for everyone. Even for those who do go in that direction, it may not be permanent. You may find yourself called to a different career for a season. I tell young people that if the Lord has given you a gift for something—engineering, business management, making videos, or whatever it might be—pursue that, use it, and make a career out of it. And remember that the Lord often leads us into a situation for a season, and then that season ends. If you continue following him through the changing seasons, asking those two questions—"What next, Lord?" and "How can we serve you, Lord?"—even if you have uncertainty, you will also have the joy of the Lord.

We thought maybe the Lord would lead us to another overseas missions opportunity, so we looked for a chance to serve somewhere else. We pursued missionary opportunities in Hungary. It was the early 1990s. Perestroika and the collapse of the USSR seemed to be opening doors. Andrea was a first-generation Hungarian-American, and we felt strongly that the Lord would take us there. However, God never opened that door or the others we investigated. Something always came up that prevented us from going.

As we were thinking about what to do next, I got a call from my college roommate Javier. "I've got a job for you," he told me. He was working at a computer store, and they needed to hire another employee. That ended up being me. I'm thankful for that job because it gave me some experience with computers that I hadn't gotten in college and would need for future work. This was the early 1990s, and personal computers were gaining traction. So I spent my days repairing and selling Apple Macintosh computers. The Lord also had some other plans for me at that job. Few of my coworkers were Christians, so I had plenty of opportunities to talk with them about Jesus. It was like a mission field at work every day.

Your career can be a ministry to your family, to support them and provide for them. You will also have opportunities to share the Gospel with your coworkers, clients, and customers. You can show them and tell them how Jesus has transformed your life and how he can transform theirs. While you are working, you can serve in your church. Be an elder, teach the kids' Sunday school class, or help prepare for the worship service.

As you ask the Lord, "How can I serve you?" you may find that the answer is full-time ministry. Or you may find that he is giving you opportunities to serve in your current career, in retirement, or as you go to school. The most important thing is to ask the question and see where the Lord points you. That will take you into the heart of his will and the best life you can live.

# 7

## Setbacks Will Happen

DID YOUR PARENTS ever talk about "growing pains"? When I was a kid, adults used to diagnose almost every unexplained discomfort as growing pains. My body was just doing the difficult work of growing and changing, they said. It wasn't very comforting. It is true, though, that change is not easy.

We go through "growing pains" in all sorts of ways in life, not just as our bodies grow, right? Whenever you transition from one thing to another—starting a new job, moving to a new town, getting married, having children, or retiring—you're going to experience pain and discomfort. Sometimes that happens over the course of years. Other times you can pinpoint a single day or moment.

February 16, 1991, was one of those days. At that time, I was working at the computer store. Andrea was at home full-time with our son Alex and was pregnant with our second child, Emily. The time had come for Emily to be born, so we excitedly drove to the hospital. I needed to stop at work on our way. While I was there, my boss unexpectedly called me in for a quick chat. "We've had a slowdown," he said. "We're going to have to reduce our staff." I was going to be one of those "reductions." If you've ever received that kind of news, you know how hard it hits you. It's unreal. And I was literally on my way to the hospital for the birth of my daughter. I walked back to the car wondering, *Do I tell Andrea this news right now or not?*

Emily was born that day, so I found out I was losing my job on my daughter's birthday. By the way, Emily's name means "industrious." God worked it out, though. I was able to stay home with Andrea, our son Alex, and our newborn daughter. In hindsight, that was an unexpected blessing for our family for that season. That experience could have filled me with bitterness and anger. Instead, God gave me the grace to look for him in the uncertainty of that season. I believe the lessons of my childhood had trained me to look for God when things got chaotic. I didn't know what was going on, but he did. He would work it all out for my good, and I would see it eventually.

## Professional Opportunities Come and Go

Three weeks later, I got my first engineering job. My career advanced to match my growing family at home. Two years into my work at the engineering firm (and with another addition to the family—Anastasia, whose name means "of the springtime" and "of the resurrection"), I decided to take the next step: I went back to school to earn my master's degree in civil engineering. That would mean more professional opportunities and more earning potential for the future. My sense of calling to ministry was still there, but the Lord had me in this career for now, so I kept moving along that path. I got into a civil engineering master's program at UVA and continued working at the same time. When I graduated in 1995, I carried my two-month-old son Christian across the stage with me. (Little did I know he would be receiving his own master's diploma from UVA twenty-three years later.)

A year later, in 1996, I had a dream. In that dream, I lost my job. For a thirty-year-old adult with a wife and four kids, that's a pretty scary dream, right? In the weeks that followed, my dream came true. My boss told me our company was merging and they'd be letting some people go. I was in mid-management, and my department was going to be phased out.

There was plenty to worry about. I was the primary breadwinner at that point. On top of that, this was a blow to my pride and sense of identity. I saw myself as a successful career engineer. I was going places, and I was going to earn a good living and support my family well. I was a professional. Now, all of a sudden, I was expendable. I didn't have a job. I had been let go. It was like the grown-up version of the death of my football dream. The same kind of identity crisis—with so much added responsibility on top.

But I began to pray and ask those same questions I had learned to ask before: "Lord, what's next?" and "Lord, how can I serve you?"

Looking back at that season, you could say that I had plenty of opportunities. I was young, early in my career. I had a bachelor's and a master's from a great university, plus some super experience. I could count on recommendations from people at my company. So I kept looking farther down the path I knew: engineering. I started interviewing with some other engineering firms. Some of these possibilities actually seemed promising. I learned that one firm, located about an hour away, had narrowed down their candidates to me and one other person. The pay was good; my salary could potentially double from my previous job. Things were starting to look up. Then God did something he sometimes does: he interrupted my progress and my plans.

**Follow David's Example**

At that time, we were attending church with a godly man named Bo Barredo. Bo had co-founded a missions organization called Advancing Native Missions just a few years earlier. It was a small but thriving and impactful place, full of faith and prayer. When Bo found out about my job situation, he invited me to visit ANM during this transition time. In fact, he told me, "Come spend six months with us while you are in transition." He called it a "six-month vacation." Then he said that I could wait and see where the Lord would take me next.

Bo's invitation touched a desire in my heart. Andrea and I had never completely let go of our vision of serving the Lord through missions, even though we hadn't succeeded in finding a long-term missions position overseas. I still tried to make the most of every opportunity I had to serve the Lord: We were very involved in our local church. I had completed a ministry training course offered by our denomination. During my time at the computer company, I had witnessed to everyone there. The same thing happened at the engineering firm.

When I visited ANM for the first time, I was immediately drawn to the love and vision of the people as they pursued their goal, which was found in Jesus' words in Matthew 24:14: "This gospel of the kingdom will be preached in all the world as a testimony to all nations, and then the end will come." The missions paradigm of encouraging, equipping, and advocating for native missionaries so they could finish the task of "reaching the unreached" was brand new to us, but it made sense. We had assumed that we had to go overseas ourselves to be involved in global missions. But the tens of thousands of dollars it would have cost to send Andrea and me to serve in another country with a different language and culture could instead support many native pastors doing the same work more effectively. We could multiply ourselves and our resources many times over by loving and standing with local indigenous pastors who were already there serving the Lord.

It was clear from the beginning that I could have a full-time role at ANM if I wanted it. In terms of my sense of calling, there was a rush of excitement. Andrea and I could finally make a big step toward the vision we felt God had given us all those years ago. Then again, this would be a huge change, and not only in the kind of work I would be doing. There was also my family's financial well-being to consider. Nonprofits typically don't pay as well as for-profit companies. ANM went even further: staff members raised their own support through donations. I had four kids. We all liked to eat. We appreciated having a roof over our heads. I've always said that my first ministry is to my family. I was about to double my salary in engineering, with the potential for more as I advanced. I was still relatively early in my career and getting ready to fly. In the next five years, I could earn my professional engineer license and increase my earnings even more. I mean, a licensed professional gets paid $10,000 to stamp a blueprint!

This was a difficult decision. In a way, it was a choice between the known and the unknown, or even between security and faith. I had a sense that following the Lord's call would lead me down the path of true peace and joy, but there were definitely nagging questions that kept me from moving forward. The question that kept repeating in my head most often was this: "God, will you take care of us if we do this?" I'm sure you've asked that question too, or some version of it. God seems to be calling you down a certain path. You might be confident that it's the right thing to do. Or you might just have a subtle sense that it's the way God would have you go. But not everything is clear. There are gaps in the plan, details left out, and questions unanswered. What do you do?

I followed the example of one of my biblical heroes, someone else who found himself following God into uncertain situations: David. There's this phrase in the Old Testament: "inquired of the Lord." Multiple times, in 1 Samuel 23, 1 Samuel 30, 2 Samuel 5, and other places it says that "David inquired of the Lord." Should he attack the Philistines or not? And the Lord would answer, "Yes! Attack!" or "No, not now. Wait."

God gave David very specific instructions. That struck me. David was a person; I'm a person. So I decided I was going "inquire of the Lord" and wait and see what the Lord said to me. I wanted to join ANM and get involved in missions in that way. I had a strong conviction that God had a special calling for Andrea and me, that he had a full-time ministry for me. I had a sense that stepping out in faith toward that calling would bring peace and purpose and joy. But again, my first ministry was to my family.

That's when God spoke to me. One night at church, our pastor invited people to come up to the altar if they had something to pray about. So I went up. "Lord, you know this is the decision I have to make," I prayed. "I really need to know: what is your perfect will for Andrea and our family?"

A brother in the church, with no knowledge of my prayer request, came and laid his hand on me and said, "Oliver, God has called you to go down this path. He will provide for you, and he will provide for your family." That was like manna. That was Sunday night. The next morning, I gave my two weeks' notice.

Yet again, God was ending a season in my life. It was time to let go of a dream—my dream of a steady, prosperous professional life as an engineer. But God was leading me into a new adventure. During the next few months, I didn't necessarily have a quiet, confident voice inside my head saying, "I know what's coming next. This will all be easy and fine." It was definitely a time of faith-building as we raised support. There were growing pains. Looking back, I see that none of it was wasted. The Lord led me through the difficulties. And he used the lessons he had taught me earlier in life. I would do whatever was in my hands, and the Lord would take care of everything.

As I made steps toward the Lord's call, I understood that that was where I would find joy, even if I didn't find the kind of security the world seeks. Because Invincible Joy comes when you're on a faith-filled journey with the Lord.

# 8

# Big Decisions Call for
# Faith-Filled Action

YOU'RE GOING TO face multiple life-changing decisions in your life. We all do. When you're considering a decision, whether it's a career change like I was considering after I lost my job, or a marriage proposal or anything else, how do you decide when to act? Well-meaning believers often get paralyzed considering their options and wondering what the right thing to do is. As I said in the previous chapter, I believe the path of Invincible Joy is the one that takes us on an adventure with the Lord, regardless of whatever uncertainty may accompany us on that journey. Because decision making is so important, I want to unpack it a little more.

You probably know the saying, "seize the day." In Latin it is "carpe diem." The Roman poet Horace coined the phrase more than two thousand years ago, and the movie *Dead Poets Society* made it famous again in 1989. In Merriam-Webster's dictionary, you will find this meaning for "seize": "to possess or take by force." Seizing the day is about seeing an opportunity and moving with all your energy to take advantage of it. It requires decisiveness, determination, and hope. Often there is a moment of opportunity that presents itself, and then it is gone. You may have to act quickly.

There is joy in seizing the right opportunity and following the Lord into the unknown. But you might appreciate some more guidance on when to seize an opportunity. There are plenty of things you can devote your time and energy to every day. How do you know which of those opportunities you should seize? You'll know that the right moment or the right opportunity has arrived when one or more of these seven conditions is true:

1) Seize the moment when righteousness is your intention and purpose. The Lord always honors your desire to honor him. You may not know exactly how things are going to turn out. You may not know the steps between here and the end, but the Lord will take care of all of that if your desire is for righteousness. You might even make

this a daily prayer to prepare yourself to seize the moment: "Lord, I desire righteousness."

2) Seize the moment when you have perfect peace. This one is tricky. Sometimes you will have questions and doubts right up to the moment of decision. Sometimes it takes a lot of wrestling in your spirit. You may seek godly counsel from many people and still be unsure of what to do. But then at the moment of decision, when you have said yes in faith, the perfect peace of the Lord washes over you. Then you know. It can feel like a confirmation from the Lord.

3) Seize the moment when the decision involves a victory over your self, your flesh, or your self-interest. Whenever we can submit to God's will instead of following our own ways, that's a good thing. For a scripture reference, I'll turn to Romans 8 again. In verses 13 and 14, Paul writes, "For if you live according to the flesh, you will die; but if by the Spirit you put to death the misdeeds of the body, you will live. For those who are led by the Spirit of God are the children of God." Paul gives a choice here: life according to the flesh, which is actually death; or life according to the

Spirit, which involves putting the flesh to death and becoming a child of God. That seems like a clear choice, right?

4) Seize the moment when the end result glorifies God. This is one of the "five *solas*" of the Reformation, which often guide me. They are *sola scriptura* (Scripture alone), *solus Christus* (Christ alone), *sola fide* (faith alone), *sola gratia* (grace alone), and *soli Deo gloria* (glory to God alone). All five are good guides for life, but especially when considering an opportunity to take action, I find that God receiving all the glory is a great guideline.

5) Seize the moment when "there is no time to lose." Sometimes an opportunity presents itself and there is no second chance in sight. The window of opportunity is going to close any minute, and you have to act immediately. Maybe you have been house hunting and a great house finally becomes available. It's a good fit for your family's needs and for your budget, but another buyer is about to put in an offer. You need to act fast and seize the opportunity. Or maybe you've wanted to strike up a conversation with that special

someone for months, and all of a sudden there you are in the same coffee shop. That's a rare opportunity that may not come again. Seize that moment. Of course, not everything that appears urgent and timely actually is. Companies make a lot of money with the words, "limited time only," "right now," and "before it's too late." That's where the next condition comes in.

6) Seize the moment when you are following wisdom. Proverbs says that wisdom is calling in the streets. Wisdom can be defined as knowing the right thing to do at the right time. Whereas the desires of our hearts and the inputs of the world can be shifting and misleading, wisdom helps us understand what's really important. When we listen to wisdom, we can see the long-term impact of our decisions and actions. Sometimes that wisdom comes from scripture, sometimes directly from the Lord, or sometimes through godly counsel. Proverbs 15:22 says, "Plans fail for lack of counsel, but with many advisers they succeed."

Do you have godly counselors you can call on when you need help making a decision? I encourage you to cultivate those relationships, perhaps with an older brother or sister in the Lord. It is so valuable to be able to spend some time with someone who also loves the Lord and is a little further along in the journey of faith than you are. They may have experiences that you can learn from. And remember James 1:5, which says, "If any of you lacks wisdom, you should ask God, who gives generously to all without finding fault, and it will be given to you." If you are seeking wisdom, God will provide it.

7) Finally, seize the moment when you hear from God. This might happen through an audible word from the Lord. That doesn't happen very often to most people. You might, though, hear from the Lord in another way. The Lord might speak to you through the Bible or a pastor or a godly friend. You might hear a word from the Lord in your heart during your prayer time or worship or Bible study. If it lines up with scripture, take it and run with it!

I shared earlier about the time when I was inquiring of the Lord about whether to join the staff at Advancing Native Missions or to continue seeking work in engineering. When the brother from the church prayed over me and told me that the Lord would take care of my family, that clinched my decision for me. I knew what to do, and I did it right away. By the way, our fifth and final child, Michael, was born to us about five years after I joined ANM. Our quiver was full.

In Galatians 6:10, Paul says, "As we have opportunity, let us do good to all people, especially to those who belong to the family of believers." To seize the opportunity, you have to be aware of it, and you have to look for it. I encourage you to make this something you repeat to yourself daily: "As I have opportunity." Just doing that will cause a change in your mindset. Almost everything becomes an opportunity. Every moment is filled with potential. When one or more of the conditions above is true, and you believe an opportunity is a gift from the Lord, take it and move forward. In that place of boldness, uncertainty, and faith, you will experience Invincible Joy.

**Follow Through**

When I was playing football, I learned that if you want to win, you have to get on the field. And if you are going to be on the field, you'd better run fast and hit hard.

You have to be reckless. Anything less will put you on the sidelines of the game. You don't win games on the sidelines.

Once you've decided to seize the moment and take action, do it with all your heart, as Paul says in Colossians 3:23: "Whatever you do, work at it with all your heart, as working for the Lord, not for human masters." You've probably heard the saying, "If something is worth doing, it's worth doing well." I believe that's true, and here's an upgrade on that saying, inspired by Colossians: "If something is worth doing, it's worth doing with all your heart." Don't hold back. Invincible Joy comes when you are in the situation where failure seems likely or even certain, because that's where you are entirely dependent on God. And God delivers.

Here's a cautionary tale from 2 Kings 13: Jehoash, king of Israel, heard that the prophet Elisha was dying. Elisha was a powerful figure in Israel. I'm sure Joash wondered what was going to happen to his kingdom if Elisha was no longer there. Maybe he wanted to talk to Elisha about the future, hear some final message from the Lord, or gain the Lord's favor by honoring his prophet. He saw this as a crucial moment in the history of his kingdom.

When Jehoash arrived, he found Elisha on his deathbed. Jehoash wept and cried out, "My father! My father!" he cried. "The chariots and horsemen of Israel!" He understood the significance of this man to his kingdom. He was more valuable than the entire army! Then Elisha gave Jehoash some instructions that might sound strange to you. He was supposed to take a bow and some arrows and then shoot an arrow out the open window. I hope he looked first to make sure no one was there! After he shot the arrow, Elisha said that the Lord would give Jehoash victory over the Arameans. Wow! Wouldn't that be a boost to Jehoash's faith?

Well, as a follow-up, Elisha gave the king another seemingly small task: take the remaining arrows and strike the ground with them. So Jehoash grabbed the arrows and he struck the ground three times. I don't know why three seemed to be the right number of times to Jehoash, but Elisha had something to say about it: "You should have struck the ground five or six times; then you would have defeated Aram and completely destroyed it. But now you will defeat it only three times."

Why did Elisha rebuke Jehoash? He failed to seize the God-given moment. He didn't act with enough vigor or enthusiasm. He wasn't wholehearted. Jehoash had just received an incredible sign from shooting the first arrow out the window. His mind could have been open to the possibilities of what the Lord would do next. But his half-hearted attempt cost him and the people who depended on him.

When faced with an opportunity, some people see it as merely something to get through. The potential is unknown. It could be a waste of time and energy. They do only what seems necessary to get through it, then move on. Others see opportunities as open-ended. Yes, the potential is unknown; it could be a small thing, but it could also be huge. It's time to seize it and strike while the iron is hot, as the saying goes—not just once, but until the iron isn't hot anymore!

History books are filled with people who saw an opportunity and seized it, whether for good or for evil. One of my favorite examples is the Founding Fathers of the United States, who seized the day and struck with everything they had—all their intelligence, determination, resources, and physical ability. Not only that, but they also inspired many others to follow them toward independence. That's taking full advantage of the opportunity.

When you cook a meal for your family, cook with all your heart. When you do your job at work, do it with all your heart. When you take care of your friend who is sick, take care of him or her with all your heart. When you pray, pray with all your heart. When you play ball with your kids, play ball with all your heart. When you worship the Lord, worship with all your heart. Of course, we can bring our best to every opportunity and every task, but we trust the Lord for the results. And giving your whole heart to these things might require you to be more careful about what you decide to do. It's not possible to do everything, but I believe it's possible to do everything you choose to do with your whole heart.

**The Legacy of Seizing the Moment**

I'll close with a short story from Acts 9:3–14 for your encouragement. Paul (called Saul) is on his way to Damascus to persecute the Christians there. Jesus confronts him on the road, blinds him, and sends him into Damascus to wait. Meanwhile, a believer named Ananias sits at home with no idea what's about to happen. Maybe he is just enjoying a few moments of quiet time with the Lord. All of a sudden, God speaks to him: "Go to the house of Judas on Straight Street and ask for a man from Tarsus named Saul, for he is praying. In a vision he has seen a man named Ananias come and place his hands on him to restore his sight."

Ananias responds, "Lord, I have heard many reports about this man and all the harm he has done to your holy people in Jerusalem. And he has come here with authority from the chief priests to arrest all who call on your name." Ananias knows Paul's reputation. He knows Paul's purpose in Damascus. He knows he is Paul's target. Ananias has a good reason to be afraid and uncertain. This is one of those crucial moments of decision. Will Ananias take a pass, or will he seize it in faith?

The next thing we know is that Ananias shows up at the house where Paul is staying and greets him in this beautiful way: "Brother Saul." Ananias trusted the Lord. He believed that the Lord could bring good out of evil. He believed that God could do the miraculous. He believed that God would watch over him in this potentially dangerous situation. And he seized the moment.

Now, maybe God would have sent someone else to see Paul if Ananias had refused. But because he said yes, Ananias got to participate in the dramatic conversion and calling of one of the greatest witnesses to the Gospel in history, the author of Romans and about a quarter of the words in the New Testament. Paul includes Ananias in his testimony to the crowds in Jerusalem in Acts 22. We don't know what else Ananias did, but even if we only consider this one episode in his life—what a legacy!

How about you? Will you "seize the moment"? Will you rise above yourself, have faith for the future, trust God in the unknown, and claim Invincible Joy?

# 9

# Every Day Counts

IN MAY 1961, President John F. Kennedy declared a commitment to landing a person on the moon before the end of the decade. It was an ambitious move. Though it wasn't necessarily inspired by the Lord's work in his heart, it was the kind of "into the unknown" move that brings Invincible Joy into our lives when we step out in faith with God. For that reason, I want to share a little more about it with you.

In 1994, Jim Collins and Jerry Porras wrote a book called *Built to Last: Successful Habits of Visionary Companies*. One of the markers of success they identified based on their research was setting Big, Hairy, Audacious Goals, or BHAGs for short. Well, President Kennedy definitely set a BHAG. It seemed out of reach—too big, too ambitious.

For the next eight years, NASA engineers, scientists, astronauts, and other team members worked toward that goal. There were countless research and development projects, multiple unmanned and manned test flights, and tens of thousands of people working toward this one goal of putting a man on the moon. The project lasted more than 2,000 workdays.

Here's the point I want to make for you right now: only one of those 2,000+ days saw Neil Armstrong take the first step on the moon. One day out of 2,000. But each of those 2,000 days was necessary to get to the ultimate goal.

To achieve your goals and finish the tasks before you, you have to do your part today. Win the day, day after day, and you'll win the ultimate victory. Imagine if those NASA engineers working on the life support system had decided that their work didn't matter as much because it wasn't the day of the moon landing. Or if the astronauts hadn't trained their bodies for space because it wasn't the day of the moon landing. Or if the mission command hadn't tested all the communications systems because it wasn't the day of the moon landing. Every day counts, because every day counts toward the total.

**Process Prepares Us for Victory**

So how do you win the day? I like to tell myself that process develops habits, habits win the day today, and winning the day wins the victory. You may have heard Henry Ford's saying, "The process is as important as the outcome." That's true because God cares about how we do things—our character. Ford's saying is also true because the process is what determines the outcome. If we're not focused on the right things today and investing our time, energy, and resources into the right things today, we can't expect to end up where we want to be in the future.

Here's another example from my own personal experience, and maybe yours too. When you play sports, every day isn't game day. I remember when we started "two-a-days" for football in the summer. Those were two practices a day in the heat of August. We were living and breathing football on those days. But the first game was still weeks away. It's easy to lose heart five hours into a grueling day of football practice when it's ninety degrees outside and there's no game at the end of the week. But it's those practice days that made us ready for the games later in the season, and ultimately—for a few teams—playoffs and championships at the end of the season.

81

Like I said, process prepares us for victory. That's not just true in sports and the space race. It's true in the life of faith too. I'll show you what I mean. When we turn to Jesus every day in prayer, Bible reading, and the other processes and habits that build us up, we start to see at least five things happening in our lives:

1) We become more like Jesus. Romans 6:22 says, "But now that you have been set free from sin and have become slaves of God, the benefit you reap leads to holiness, and the result is eternal life." In God's service, we become holy. 1 Corinthians 1:30 says, "It is because of him that you are in Christ Jesus, who has become for us wisdom from God—that is, our righteousness, holiness and redemption."

2) We believe more. In Mark 9:23, Jesus says, "Everything is possible for one who believes." Part of God's process is for us to grow in faith, knowing that God is who he says he is, that he can do what he promises.

3) We pray more. In 1 Thessalonians 5:16-18, Paul tells the church to "Rejoice always, pray

continually, give thanks in all circumstances; for this is God's will for you in Christ Jesus."

4) We love more. You know 1 Corinthians 13, "the Love Chapter." I'm sure you've heard it read at many weddings. When we are abiding in Christ, our love becomes more like the love Paul describes in this chapter: patient, kind, not envious, not boasting, not proud, and so on.

5) We expect more. Ephesians 3:20 talks about God as the one "who is able to do immeasurably more than all we ask or imagine, according to his power that is at work within us." God's process includes us turning to him in faith and believing that he will do great things in our lives for his glory and our good.

These things build on each other. As we turn our attention to Jesus, believe more, pray more, love more, and expect more, we find ourselves doing these things even more. And more victories follow. 1 Corinthians 15:57–58 says, "But thanks be to God, who gives us the victory through our Lord Jesus Christ. Therefore, my beloved brothers, be steadfast, immovable, always abounding in the work of the Lord, knowing that in the Lord your labor is not in vain."

One final quick word of clarification: Of course, the ultimate victory is already won through our Lord Jesus Christ. Practically, though, we still have to fight the battles. However, the scriptures tell us that the Lord even fights the battles on our behalf! So how can we lose? Remember Romans 8:31: "If God is for us, who can be against us?" I encourage you to trust the Lord for today, and as you do that, to trust him for the victory to come.

# 10

## Joy Is Meant to Be Shared

SO YOU'VE EXPERIENCED salvation, reconciliation with God, the peace of Christ in your heart, Invincible Joy in the midst of the struggles of life. Is that everything God has planned for you?

The truth is that many Christians have an incomplete walk with the Lord. Their vision for a life following Jesus begins and ends with salvation from sin. Yes, Jesus died and rose from the dead so that you would be saved from your sins and enjoy eternal life with him. He redeemed you when you could not save yourself. That is definitely at the heart of the Lord's desire for you. Jesus wants to redeem you from darkness, hopelessness, sin, brokenness, and death. But there's more.

Let's go back to football for a minute. What if you trained every day with your team, did preseason workouts, lifted weights, ran sprints, memorized plays, and practiced routes, but never played a game? You practiced and prepared, and then the coach said, "Okay. Good work. See you next season." Now compare that to how we view our life with the Lord. I don't mean that you and I are doing all the work. The Lord is sovereign and gracious, and he alone does the saving work in our lives. But what if all we ever did was *prepare* to play the game, and never actually played? When God saves us, that's not the end. He has a further purpose for our lives. He wants us in the game, playing all-out, pursuing the victory.

When I need a reminder of this, I turn to one of my favorite passages in the whole Bible: Ephesians 2:1–10. In verse 10, Paul says, "We are God's handiwork, created in Christ Jesus to do good works, which God prepared in advance for us to do." Paul emphasizes that God did an incredible saving work in your life. He did it all, and he gets the glory. That's the heart of verses 1–9. Then Paul shows us the next step, the follow-up: by accomplishing this saving work, God has prepared us to do good works for him, and he has prepared the good works for us. Again, I want to say this carefully because some Christians get confused by the whole "works" thing. We're not saved by works—Paul is abundantly clear about that in verse 9 ("not by works"). But God has prepared us to do good works. He has given us an assignment. In other words, the Christian life simply isn't complete without getting involved in God's purpose for us. Our purpose is to advance his purpose.

But what is that purpose? You can look at a lot of scriptural references to get an answer to that question. Deuteronomy 6:5 gives us the Greatest Commandment: "Love the LORD your God with all your heart and with all your soul and with all your strength." In Matthew 22:37–40, Jesus amplifies and expands on this: "'Love the Lord your God with all your heart and with all your soul and with all your mind.' This is the first and greatest commandment. And the second is like it: 'Love your neighbor as yourself.' All the Law and the Prophets hang on these two commandments."

The Westminster Shorter Catechism asks a series of questions to help Christians understand their faith and calling. One of these questions is, "What is the chief end of man?" The answer the Catechism gives is "To glorify God and to enjoy him forever." You can see how that draws on the theme of the Greatest Commandment.

I'll sum it up this way: When God gives you the gift of Invincible Joy as you experience his presence and care in the ups and downs of life, he also desires that you share it. It's supposed to overflow and lead to transformation for others. I believe the Lord has specific ways that he wants to connect you to that purpose. They might involve sharing the Gospel with your coworkers or your next-door neighbor. God might be calling you to love and glorify him by leading worship in your local church or teaching Sunday school. The possibilities are endless, but the point is that the Lord wants you to have an impact for Christ in the world around you.

**The Example of Jesus**

My greatest mentor and my predecessor as president of Advancing Native Missions, Bo Barredo, often says, "The best life is a life lived for others." You've probably heard some version of that before. There is plenty of scripture to back it up.

We're selfish people by nature, right? We like to have things our way, on our schedule, at a good price, with a smile. Whether consciously or subconsciously, we tend to follow this motto: "The best life is the life where everyone is living for me." Of course, that's not what we see Jesus model for us. I like to look back at Philippians 2 whenever I need a reminder of the kind of life Jesus lived:

*So if there is any encouragement in Christ, any comfort from love, any participation in the Spirit, any affection and sympathy, complete my joy by being of the same mind, having the same love, being in full accord and of one mind. Do nothing from selfish ambition or conceit, but in humility count others more significant than yourselves. Let each of you look not only to his own interests, but also to the interests of others. Have this mind among yourselves, which is yours in Christ Jesus, who, though he was in the form of God, did not count equality with God a thing to be grasped, but emptied himself, by taking the form of a servant, being born in the likeness of men. And being found in human form, he humbled himself by becoming obedient to the point of death, even death on a cross. Therefore God has highly exalted him and bestowed on him the name that is above every name, so that at the name of Jesus every knee should bow, in heaven and on earth and under the earth, and every tongue confess that Jesus Christ is Lord, to the glory of God the Father (ESV).*

One of the key phrases for me in that passage is "emptied himself." Jesus had everything. He was on the throne. He had equality with God. He had all the power and authority. And he poured it all out for our sake. He emptied himself of glory to become a servant. He even went through the humility of birth and infancy.

Jesus modeled that humility throughout his life. The story of the Last Supper in John's Gospel is a perfect example. According to custom, the servant, or the lowliest person in the group, was supposed to wash the feet of all the guests. In John 13, we see Jesus getting up from the table, taking off his outer clothes, and wrapping himself with a towel. Imagine how surprised the disciples must have been as they watched him. He got water and a basin and started to wash their feet. You know Peter's response: "Lord, do you wash my feet? ... You shall never wash my feet." Wow! Jesus' actions were so unexpected that Peter rebukes him!

What Jesus says a little later is so beautiful: "Do you understand what I have done to you? You call me Teacher and Lord, and you are right, for so I am. If I then, your Lord and Teacher, have washed your feet, you also ought to wash one another's feet. For I have given you an example, that you also should do just as I have done to you. Truly, truly, I say to you, a servant is not greater than his master, nor is a messenger greater than the one who sent him. If you know these things, blessed are you if you do them." This is the kind of God we serve, and he tells us that we are to follow his example in serving others.

Those two passages are part of my inspiration for how I interact with others, whether in the organization I lead or in my family or in any other situation. I like to follow the way of "servant leadership." Humility is one essential part of this way of living and leading. The other key piece is a question: "How can I be part of the answer to prayers in this situation?" Often we find ourselves in situations where we are asking God to do something to change the way things are. Or we know that others are praying prayers asking God to change something. Well, what if God intends for you and me to be part of the solution?

As I've said before, authority and power come from God, and all glory belongs to him. God chooses to work through people, though, and sometimes he calls us to make an impact in someone's life in Jesus' name. There's a passage in James 2 where we are told that it's not enough to just say "be blessed" to those in need. We are supposed to actually do something to help them. Of course, you can't solve every problem. A good start may be to ask a question of the Lord when you bring a request to him in prayer: "Lord, is there some way you want me to be involved in your answer to this prayer?"

Be warned: if you do this, you will get involved in things you never expected to be involved in. It may take you out of your comfort zone, but it will always take you into God's will. That's the best place to be. I'll give you an example of a couple who became part of God's answer to a prayer. In this case, it was their own prayer, and it took them on an adventure that transformed their lives and the lives of many others.

In 2017, I traveled to India as part of a team from Advancing Native Missions, where I was chief operating officer at the time. We went to a certain village in northern India. The state of Jammu and Kashmir in the north is the only one of India's twenty-eight states and eight territories that has a Muslim majority. Hinduism is the major religion in most of India. Decades ago, a young husband and wife, P. M. and Christie Thomas, were living in south India and working as teachers. They were Christians. When they looked around them, they saw that Christianity was common in their part of India, but in the north there were very few Christians. So they started praying, "Lord, send someone to north India to preach the Gospel."

Well, God told P. M. and Christie to go. They experienced a sacred moment when the Lord presented them with an opportunity. It seemed to be beyond their capacity. It would certainly take them out of their comfort zone. But it checked all the boxes for seizing the moment: it came from a righteous desire, the Lord would be glorified, and it involved a victory over themselves. And it brought joy to them and so many others as they fulfilled their calling.

First they went to a city of about one million people. P. M. learned that there were three churches in that city and said, "The work is already happening here. I'll go to the next village." So they moved on and started a ministry in a place where there were no other ministries and no churches. That was almost fifty years ago. Multiple ministries and thousands of missionaries have come out of their work. I'm confident that hundreds of thousands of people have heard the Gospel because of their faithfulness to say yes to God's call.

During my visit to India forty years later, I was honored to step inside the 10x20 hut P. M. and Christie built and lived in when they first moved there. The doorway was about five feet high. My son, Alex, was with me. He's taller than I am, and he had to practically crawl through. It felt like holy ground to stand inside that simple dwelling. This couple answered the call, seized the moment, and endured the hardships. Thousands of lives were transformed for eternity because of it.

Talk about becoming part of the answer to a prayer—their own prayer! What situations might God be ready to use you in?

# 11

## The Entire World Needs What You Have

GOD WORKS IN each person's life to bring salvation, peace, and reconciliation with him. As a seven-year-old boy, I found joy and hope in Jesus thanks to the testimony of my Grandma Lilly and my mom, Carol. I knew that I was sinful and needed a Savior. I knew that God wanted to sanctify me and grow me into the likeness of Jesus. He also called me to share what he's given to me with others. As I mentioned before, I believe that's part of God's calling and vision for each Christian—to spread the Good News of Jesus with those around us who still need to hear and receive it.

It gets even bigger than that. Look around: the world is full of war, poverty, crime, broken families, broken relationships, and every kind of evil you can imagine. I bet you're like me in that some days it just seems overwhelming. You ask God, "Lord, how much longer? When will you step in and solve all these problems?" At least twelve of the Psalms have this key question at their core: "How long?" Psalm 94 is a great example:

> O Lord, God of vengeance,
> O God of vengeance, shine forth!
> Rise up, O judge of the earth;
> repay to the proud what they deserve!
> O Lord, how long shall the wicked,
> how long shall the wicked exult?
> They pour out their arrogant words;
> all the evildoers boast.
> They crush your people, O Lord,
> and afflict your heritage.
> They kill the widow and the sojourner,
> and murder the fatherless;
> and they say, "The Lord does not see;
> the God of Jacob does not perceive."

The psalmist looks around and sees all the wickedness, just as you and I do, and is almost at the point of despair. It seems that evil is in charge of the world. People are opposing the Lord and his plans at every turn. It seems that there is a continual slide away from God's will and purposes.

One thing I appreciate about this Psalm is that it puts hope in the proper place. The psalmist doesn't say that he is going to rise up and put everything in order. He doesn't even call on others to join him in fixing the problems. He doesn't say, "I can't wait until everyone teams up to solve these issues. How long until all my people work together on this?" His hope isn't in his own righteousness and ability, and it's not in the people's righteousness and ability. Neither is ours. Our hope is in God's righteousness and his power.

On my best days I don't do everything right, even in my own little sphere of influence. There's no way I'm going to bring an end to all the suffering and evil around me, much less all the problems the world faces. No, the world needs something much greater than Oliver. The world needs the almighty Savior, whose name is Jesus. I realize that may seem simple and obvious, but as believers, we need to declare with conviction, "God, we need you."

## Invincible Joy for a Chaotic World

Since I joined the staff of Advancing Native Missions in 1996, Matthew 24:14 has been a key verse for me. In this passage, Jesus is telling his disciples about all the hardships that are going to come, not just in their individual lives, but also for the entire world. The world will experience wars, famines, persecution, and more. These things are happening now. We're no strangers to this kind of hardship, right? We recognize the truth of what Jesus is saying.

But then in the midst of the bad news, Jesus shares a message of Invincible Joy: "And this gospel of the kingdom will be preached in all the whole world as a testimony to all nations, and then the end will come." That's a reassuring promise. In the midst of all the chaos and catastrophe, the Good News is going to keep spreading. God is going to keep doing his work among the nations until the whole world is aware of it. That is when the end will come. And it's a good end, when Jesus will make everything right and fully establish his reign. That's when the suffering and chaos of the world will finally be resolved. Only then. The return of Jesus is the end of the world's suffering and trouble. The answer to the world's problems is Jesus returning and fully establishing his kingdom. Ultimate restoration. Ultimate reconciliation. True peace. Invincible Joy.

People, even believers, put their hope in so many things. They think if more people understood the dangers of climate change, if we could make better economic decisions as a society, or if the right political party came to power, our problems would be solved. None of that is going to lead to the end of evil and suffering. That will happen only when Jesus returns. And Jesus promised that he will return after the Gospel has been preached to all nations.

That makes it pretty clear what we can do to make the world a better place, right? Share the Gospel with those who have not yet heard. Help the Good News of Jesus Christ get to places where it has never been heard before. Make disciples of all nations until every nation has a strong Gospel witness.

By the way, many Christians misunderstand the word "nations" in the New Testament. Jesus isn't talking about the political boundaries of the world. He's not telling his disciples to preach the Gospel in Saudi Arabia and Mexico and the Czech Republic. In the Bible, "nation" means *ethnos*, or a group of people who share a language and a culture. That's often called a people group. In every country today, there may be dozens or even hundreds of people groups. And Jesus wants every one of those people groups to hear the Gospel.

According to Jesus' words, we have the privilege of taking part in that mission. Our goal is to speed his return by taking the Gospel to more people groups who haven't yet heard it. The return of Jesus will be the greatest event in history aside from his resurrection. And you and I get to be part of bringing it about by advancing the Gospel to people who have never heard it before.

Lately, God has been emphasizing the urgency of his purpose to me: "Complete the Great Commission. It's time." It's been 2,000 years since Jesus stood on a mountaintop with his disciples and told them: "All authority in heaven and on earth has been given to me. Therefore go and make disciples of all nations, baptizing them in the name of the Father and of the Son and of the Holy Spirit, and teaching them to obey everything I have commanded you. And surely I am with you always, to the very end of the age." As I've mentioned before, this is not a one-man show. The mission is for all of us who follow Jesus. We have a responsibility as Christ's followers to join him in the work. That can start small.

## Start Small and See What God Does

In 2003, I was in central Russia. We were so far out from Moscow and the other big cities that it felt like a no-man's land. I was there for my work with Advancing Native Missions to meet some local Russian ministry workers who were striving to plant churches. You see, there are still thousands of villages scattered around Russia that don't have any kind of church. So this ministry that ANM partners with was sending out small teams to evangelize, to start small groups, and to eventually start churches in these villages.

In one town we visited, I met a young Russian missionary named Andrew. He was one of the many young people working to start new churches. He was so humble and unassuming, and his attitude displayed Christlikeness to me. Andrew told me, "I get up in the morning, kiss my wife goodbye, take my guitar, and walk five miles to town. When I get there, I sit in the square and play music. People come and talk to me, and I tell them about Jesus. Then, when it gets dark, I walk home."

This guy was in his twenties and had a wife and two toddlers at home. And he was faithfully being a witness to whoever he could in this town where people hadn't had a chance to hear about Jesus.

I thought, *How can I help?* When I asked the leader of this Russian ministry, he told me, "Well, if you could help him get a used car for $2,500, it would speed things up. He wouldn't have to walk the five miles both ways. He could do all his work, get home before dark, and spend more time with his wife and kids." That was a light-bulb moment for me. Here was a young Russian missionary, joyful and passionate for the Gospel, who could have an impact that I never could for his fellow Russians. And all he needed for his ministry to be even more effective and sustainable was a used car. When I got back to the States, ANM told people about that need and got it taken care of, along with others for these faithful Russian believers. It was a perfect example of believers in one place partnering with believers in another place to accomplish the Lord's work. One plants, another waters, and the Lord gives the increase.

There was so much joy for me in that moment. God allowed me to step into a less-than-ideal situation and bring his blessing and provision. That's Invincible Joy. This also tied in with the kingdom principle I mentioned before and that I've found to be true in my life: You can be part of the answer to the prayers of someone else. In other words, you can be part of fulfilling someone else's dream. God often uses people like you or me to show up and meet a need or to encourage or guide someone in the right direction. It empowers that person to take the next step in the direction God is calling him to go in. He is blessed, we are blessed, and God gets the glory.

You and I are called to be the "faithful servant" in Matthew 24:45–46: "Who then is the faithful and wise servant, whom the master has put in charge of the servants in his household to give them their food at the proper time? It will be good for that servant whose master finds him doing so when he returns."

And when we commit to that mission, we help the Gospel get to the last unreached places on earth. Once that happens, Jesus will return as he promised. Then the end will come, the solution to all the world's problems.

# 12

## Leave a Legacy of Joy

WHAT DOES SUCCESS look like? People answer that question in so many different ways. Those answers might be about money, children, fame, relationships, or many other things. The same person might even give different answers at different times in his life. As we near the end of this book, I want to share a few thoughts on what I believe success truly means. It has to do with the kind of legacy you will leave behind.

My dad's family, the Ashers, were poor, uneducated, law-breaking, and violent. They always seemed to be fighting. As a child, I witnessed my uncle stab and cut into the belly of another uncle, whose belt saved him from worse injury or even death. My wife, Andrea, first experienced the chaos of my family early in our marriage when she was pregnant with our firstborn, Alex. We went to my grandpa's funeral, and all the uncles and aunts were there. One uncle was released from jail for the occasion. He was serving time for arson. That night, after the service, we gathered at Grandma's trailer. All of a sudden, I saw one inebriated uncle chasing my dad with a shotgun. He pointed it directly at Dad's chest before my brother and I were able to wrestle it away from him. Andrea gathered the small children and hurried them to a back room for safety. My aunt fired another gun into the air to stop the chaos.

So, you see, my family didn't have a legacy of seeking God's plans for our lives. But because of the Lord's work in my grandma and my mom, a new legacy was being formed. Because of them, I knew God had a plan for my life. I didn't know what it was, but just knowing that much gave me hope.

Mark Batterson writes about dreams within dreams. One person's dream is born out of another person's dream. It's a ripple effect, part of someone's legacy. Only God knows how far those ripple effects will go. My grandma had a dream of telling everyone she knew about the God she loved. That birthed a dream in my mom to see her children come to faith in the Lord and to do something for his glory. My dream of following Jesus deeper and deeper into his purpose for the world and for my life grew out of Mom's dream for us. So when I look back at my family, even as I am aware of all the brokenness and chaos and darkness that surrounded us, what really catches my attention is the faithfulness of my mom and grandma. I look back in gratitude and wonder and awe at what God did in our family.

Today I like to think of my story as the story of 2 Timothy 1:5. Paul says to his protégé, Timothy, about his legacy of faith: "I am reminded of your sincere faith, which first lived in your grandmother Lois and in your mother Eunice and, I am persuaded, now lives in you also." I have a debt of gratitude to my mother and grandmother for sharing the Gospel with me. I shared that same Gospel with my own children, and as they start to raise their own families, they will share the Gospel with their children. The legacy of faith continues!

**What Will You Treasure Most?**

As I write this, I'm looking back on more than fifty years of life and almost fifty years of following Jesus. I excelled at football and left my poor, uneducated family background behind for a scholarship and an education at a top-tier university. I worked as an engineer and earned a master's degree. Now I'm the president of a growing nonprofit organization serving the Lord in global missions. But when I consider my greatest treasures, what comes to mind isn't an accomplishment or a career success. Those are all signs of the Lord's grace and goodness, but what really fills my heart is the fact that I've been on this incredible journey with God, and he has taken care of me and my family through it all.

God made it clear to me early on that if I would follow him and take my family along with me, he would take care of all our needs. Looking at my kids now, I believe the evidence is there: my five children love and support each other; they are married to wonderful, godly spouses; two of them have children so far; all are successfully pursuing careers; and most importantly, all are serving the Lord.

Here's one of the things I treasure most: As part of my work with Advancing Native Missions, I have the privilege of traveling to other countries to see firsthand the missions work taking place. Twice I have taken my oldest, Alex, with me. One of those trips was to Mongolia in 2015. There, we met the Korean missionary who had almost single-handedly ignited the growth of the Mongolian church after the fall of communism in the early 1990s. Since he started making disciples in that country, the number of believers skyrocketed from fewer than ten in 1992 to well over 50,000 today. We visited a number of different Mongolian churches during our trip there, and those believers are on fire for the Lord! What a blessing for me to witness their passion for the Lord alongside my son.

Invincible Joy is being in the Lord's presence and care in the midst of whatever the world throws at you. With that in mind, I guess I'd say that is what success looks like: going where the Lord leads and taking your loved ones with you. In other words, it's sharing Invincible Joy with those around you. I look forward to sharing more experiences like Mongolia with my children and even my grandchildren as we walk with the Lord together in the years to come.

**Gifts Are Meant to Be Shared**

I believe that when Jesus gives us a gift, it's always for us to share, and I want to close this chapter with a challenge for you. In 2 Corinthians 1, Paul calls God "the God of all comfort, who comforts us in all our troubles, so that we can comfort those in any trouble with the comfort we ourselves receive from God." Looking back at my childhood, I can see now that life was hard. I believe God took me through that kind of life so that I would have more empathy and compassion for others, especially those who are going through hard times. All humans have troubles and challenges, and I may not have experienced exactly the same things, but I can understand some of what others are experiencing and be there for them. I'm convinced that God strategically stations his people where they can be that kind of comfort and positive influence for others, sharing a taste of Invincible Joy in the midst of life's challenges. Of course, that includes family members such as my grandma and mom, but it also extends to others in your life as well.

When I was in kindergarten, I started going to Rock Elementary School across the river from where we lived. Every morning I would walk across the bridge to get to school. And every afternoon I walked home across that bridge. Sometimes my mom would have to go to work early in the morning before I left for school. She drew a picture of a clock and told me, "When the clock on the wall matches this clock, you need to walk to school." On those mornings, I would walk to and from school by myself—at five years old! Talk about a way to learn responsibility early on.

On the corner near the school lived Ms. Anderson. She was a sweet widowed lady, probably seventy years old. She was like a guardian angel to me. She often gave me an oatmeal cake or a banana on my way to school, and she would watch me on my way home after school. So even when Mom was really busy and Dad was away working, God provided Ms. Anderson. She couldn't have known that fifty years later, long after her life ended, that young boy would be telling people how God used her to bless him.

You have that same opportunity, whether with your own children or with "children in the faith," as Timothy was to Paul, or with a friend or someone else God puts in your path. Each of us has relationships within which we can pass on what the Lord has taught us. It may be a child, a younger coworker, a niece or nephew, a grandchild, or a friend. We don't usually know the long-term effect our actions or words will have on someone. The truth is, though, that God sends his people to bless, encourage, and help someone else every day. Sometimes it's only for one day; sometimes it's for a lifetime. You and I get to be that person. Just as God sent someone to be a guide to you, you can be a guide to someone else.

Who do you have that kind of relationship with already? Is there someone the Lord has placed in your life who could use encouragement, hope, and Invincible

Joy? I encourage you to pray about that and ask the Lord who he has in mind for you.

# Final Word

AS YOU GET up from reading this, I hope you feel encouraged by one indisputable fact: the Lord loves you, and therefore he has a purpose for your life.

As I said at the beginning, I don't believe my story is unique. Of course, the details are different from what you have been through. But the big picture is the same: We are all born into a broken world. We experience that brokenness in painful and sad and discouraging ways. When we turn to Jesus, we find hope and peace that the world can't take away. Amen? And when we discover God's purpose for our lives, we gain an Invincible Joy that the world doesn't understand.

It doesn't matter where you begin. God has a plan for you. He will give you hope and joy, no matter what your situation, no matter how chaotic and dark. He's the one who will shine a light in the darkness. He's also a provider—not just the physical necessities such as food and shelter, but also the spiritual nourishment you need and the people who will help guide you along the path. Look to the Lord for everything you need, and ask him how he might use you to be the guide or helper that another believer needs. God is writing a beautiful story through his people. I encourage you to find your role in that story and join in. I believe that the great purpose of our lives—my life and your life—is the Lord's purpose. And I believe that is good and exciting and fulfilling.

When I read the story of Jesus' last words in the Gospel of Matthew, I'm always encouraged by this statement: "I am with you always." That's the ultimate assurance of success, right? God is with you, all along the way. I can't think of a more reassuring statement. The God of the universe, who knows the beginning and end of everything, is with me and you at every step of the way as we walk through life. That's not to say life with the Lord isn't difficult. It often is. But it is worth it.

I'd like to close with one of the proverbs that's closest to my heart. Proverbs 16:9 says, "The heart of man plans his way, but the LORD establishes his steps" (ESV). Whenever I lead a meeting or have a time of planning or prayer with my family or just a heart-to-heart with a fellow believer, I like to conclude our time with my own paraphrase of this verse: "We make plans, but the Lord guides our steps." Then we pray together.

Right now, as you consider where you are going in life, the dreams the Lord has given you, the desires of your heart, your opportunities, your burdens, your hopes, and your fears, let the Lord guide your steps.

He is faithful and good. If he is for you, what can stand against you?

# Extra Word about Sharing Invincible Joy with the World

I READ ONCE that "Missions is God finding those whose hearts are right with him and placing them where they can make a difference for his kingdom."

For me, Jesus' words in Matthew 28:18 have played an important role in my understanding of missions, which is another way of saying sharing the Invincible Joy that Jesus puts in our hearts. In that verse, Jesus gives his disciples their final instructions: "Go and make disciples of all nations, baptizing them in the name of the Father and of the Son and of the Holy Spirit, and teaching them to obey everything I have commanded you." Christians often call this the Great Commission. These are Jesus' last words to his disciples. That gives them some extra weight, right? They are the final words of Jesus. And they sum up the mission of the church ever since: take the Good News of Jesus to every nation.

These days, it is common for Christians to assume that the Great Commission is for someone else. But Jesus isn't just talking to certain Christians or special disciples.

He doesn't say, "Peter, it's all on you. Go everywhere in the world, tell everyone the good news." Jesus gives the mission to his followers together, to all his people, to the whole church. It's a commission, an adventure, and a burden to be shared. Everyone has a role. The Great Commission will be fulfilled by all of us working together.

When Peter stood up to preach in Jerusalem in Acts 2, the other apostles stood with him. Their families and friends supported them financially. When they were in jail for the sake of Jesus, the other believers gathered to pray for them. Later in Acts, the Apostle Paul and others were sent out, prayed for, and supported by churches in Antioch, Jerusalem, and other places. When the believers in Jerusalem faced hardships and persecution, churches around the Mediterranean took responsibility and sent help.

Why? Because they were all in the mission together. The Gospel spread throughout Europe and other parts of the world because the church collectively took it upon itself to participate in the Great Commission. Some Christians went to other lands as missionaries, some paid their way, and some prayed. Famous missionaries such as William Carey and Hudson Taylor went to India, China, and other places where there wasn't yet a thriving local church. They went alone or in small groups, but they went with the prayers and the support of hundreds or thousands of Christians back home who under- stood that Jesus' Great Commission was for them too. By supporting the work of those on the frontiers of the kingdom, Christians at home could join the work instead of sitting on the sidelines. And God was there, leading the advancement of the kingdom at every step.

There's a scripture passage that has become very important to me in the past few years. I like these verses because they highlight how the body of Christ works together, and because the passage ends with the Lord getting the glory. It's 1 Corinthians 3:6–9: "I planted the seed, Apollos watered it, but God has been making it grow. So neither the one who plants nor the one who waters is anything, but only God, who makes things grow. The one who plants and the one who waters have one purpose, and they will each be rewarded according to their own labor. For we are co-workers in God's service; you are God's field, God's building." My paraphrase is: "One plants, one waters, but the Lord gives the increase."

Missions is always a cooperative effort. What a relief! I don't have to act as if it all depends on me. It's not up to me alone to deliver the Gospel to the last unreached tribe in Indonesia. That's a good thing, because I don't speak any of the Indonesian languages. And I have a wife and kids and grandkids here in the States. I also have other responsibilities here that the Lord has given me. I don't know what it's like to come to faith out of Islam (the primary religion in Indonesia). I'm not used to the climate. I don't understand the various cultures of Indonesia or what life is like on its 6,000 inhabited islands. That's the reality for many of us: for one reason or another we're not going to be the ones to cross seas, continents, and borders into places where people speak different languages, eat different foods, and worship different gods.

The good news is that after twenty centuries of missions, the seeds of the Gospel had been planted among the nations, and native Christians have begun spreading the Gospel to their own people and nearby people groups that haven't received it yet. That's what Advancing Native Missions is all about: supporting native Christians so they can do even more for God's kingdom, until everyone has a chance to hear the Gospel.

When Andrea and I were praying about whether I would join Advancing Native Missions, we started to hear stories of native believers answering the call to tell their neighbors about Jesus. One of these native missionaries I heard about was Prem Pradhan, a pioneer Christian missionary and church leader in Nepal. He was in prison for fourteen years because of his ministry. But he was so passionate that he kept sharing the Gospel with his fellow prisoners until he had practically started a church within the prison! Many of Nepal's Christians today trace their faith back to Prem Pradhan.

I was amazed at stories like that. God is fulfilling centuries of plowing and planting and watering by European and American missionaries. Churches are being led by native Christians—Brazilian pastors leading Brazilian churches, Thai pastors leading Thai churches, Mongolian pastors leading Mongolian churches—and are flourishing and multiplying.

The timing is perfect: more and more countries are closed to Americans. At least sixty countries today won't accept American missionaries, including China, North Korea, and Egypt—I can't go to one of those places and put out a sign that says I'm starting a church. On top of that, the cultural and language boundaries are still there. Each of the 7,000 ethnic groups in the world without a thriving local church has its own language or dialect, its own culture and way of doing things, its own unique flavors of religion and tradition: Kurds in Turkey, Brahmins in India, Iraqi Arabs, the Samburu-speaking peoples of Kenya, the Carabayo of Colombia, and others. But now there are local Christians in many places that are already comfortable in these cultures and confident in these languages. They're ready to serve, plant churches, and spread the kingdom of Jesus Christ to these places and peoples. And they serve at the economic level of their neighbors because that's their standard of living too.

I am not the ideal candidate to personally go reach the nations. Of course, if the Lord calls me or you, we go and serve by faith wherever he calls. But there are other ways to get involved in the Lord's mission. I can pray. I can support native Christians from Indonesia who are reaching the unreached people around them. They know the languages, they are comfortable with the cultures, and they understand Islam and maybe even used to be Muslim themselves.

I'm grateful that I get to be involved in missions full-time for my job and help other believers see that God is doing something amazing around the world and that they can be part of it. As I mentioned before, I believe God gifts people differently, and if you have gifts to use in the marketplace or in some other profession, pursue that and honor the Lord through your work.

How have you been involved in the Great Commission? Maybe you once took a missions trip to another country. Maybe you have supported a missionary from your church. Maybe you pray. For some Christians, missions hasn't even been part of their vocabulary. I hope it encourages you to know that you can have an impact in global missions wherever you live because of native missionaries serving in their own countries.

For more information about Advancing Native Missions and how you can get involved in what God is doing around the world today, visit advancingnativemissions.com. God bless.

CPSIA information can be obtained
at www.ICGtesting.com
Printed in the USA
LVHW012337191122
733278LV00037B/2147